Useful Stories for Daily Life

BY
DR. ASHOK N. SHAHANE

TOASTMASTERS HALL OF FAME INDUCTEE
and
AN EXPERIENCED PROFESSIONAL

2013

FATHER & SON
PUBLISHING, INC.

4909 North Monroe Street
Tallahassee, Florida 32303
800-741-2712

Copyright ©2013 Ashok N. Shahane

Printed in The United States of America

All rights reserved. No part of this book may be reproduced or transmitted in any form or by any means, electronic or mechanical, including photocopying and recording or by any information storage or retrieval system without prior written permission from the copyright holders.

ISBN: 978-1-935802-15-0

INTRODUCTION

A good story is a valuable tool that everybody uses in all facets of daily life. These stories not only make interactions delightful but they enlighten the environment in which the people enjoy good times. Some stories are even capable of enriching the souls of some people. During the last forty years, I've heard numerous stories that have helped me enjoy the moments of time whether it is lively conversation, presentation or a class room lecture. I have had the great privilege of telling numerous stories in both formal and informal meetings. These clean stories covered a wide range of twelve categories, including communication, educational, entertaining, environment, historical, human behavior, inspirational, miscellaneous, motivational, mysterious, philosophical, and thought-provoking. Amazingly these stories can be useful to everybody in all walks of life on this planet earth. Professors, public speakers, politicians, parents, teachers, engineers, scientists, and administrators are just few examples of professionals who can invariably use the stories to emphasize their point of view or embellish a presentation or to provide invaluable direction.

Although good stories serve well, they are easily forgotten because the average person is bombarded with so many stories daily. Over the period of time, a person is habituated to enjoy a good story momentarily and to remove it immediately from both the short and long term memories. The short-lived nature of these stories is great loss. This is unfortunate because the useful information is lost and difficult to retrieve once it is lost. Like most of people, I have spent several disappointing hours to retrieve great stories that I heard or read a few days ago. That loss of time along with great deal of frustration can be prevented if there is a methodical practice to compile these stories at the centralized place for people to access these useful stories. Unfortunately, there is no systematic method now to do that.

It is also next to impossible to gather all the stories posted on the internet. It is sometimes not even possible to search these topics because they are in unmanageable numbers. To balance these extremities, a simple effort is made in this book to compile those stories that are of general interest to the majority of society and those stories that have been tested as valuable thoughts or lessons with entertaining qualities. These stories are also collected from credible sources which are identified clearly in the reference section in addition to the places where they appear in the book. When adequate efforts failed to identify the sources, the stories are labeled as anonymous. The official permissions to use these stories in this collection have been obtained. The decisions to select the stories and categorize them in the fashion that will increase the use of these stories by the interdisciplinary professionals are that of the author. The stories are selected from a large bank of information collected by the author over the period of the last 40 years. The entertainment, education, inspiration, humor, down-to-earth common sense, patriotism, and value system are some of the criterion used by the author in selecting these stories.

This book of collection of stories is prepared by the author in his capacity as a private citizen. Therefore, these stories do not necessarily reflect the policies and viewpoints of his current and past employers.

It is my sincere hope that these 115 stories (although limited in number) become the starting point for a powerful story search for numerous occasions by people in different walks of life. With the unlimited creativity of these individuals, these stories can be used directly or indirectly with or without modifications to fit each occasion. Ultimate purpose of this effort in presenting these selected, powerful stories is to make people feel happier, joyful and to develop up-beat inspiration to lead a productive life on this planet earth.

Ashok N. Shahane
Tallahassee, Florida
September, 2012

ACKNOWLEDGEMENTS

The nature of a compilation book like this requires considerable brain-storming efforts from the people who live with you in the same environment known as "Home". I consider myself very fortunate to receive support from my wife, Meena Shahane. Not only has she asked all the challenging preliminary questions such as why, what, when, whom, where, but she provided guidance and direction when the book hobby effort was going its rough, tough and dry phases. She provided constant assistance in the multi-tasking effort in selecting the stories, editing the stories, allocating the limited resources, prioritizing numerous steps, and providing the constructive observations (criticism). It is very obvious to me that this effort would not have gone to fruition without her. Thus, Mrs. Meena Shahane is acknowledged for encouraging me to compile these stories so that they can be useful to others in many areas of their daily lives.

Mr. Craig Howard provided the consultation for putting the concepts of the book into the format that can be presented to the publisher. His valuable advice during all the phases of this book is greatly appreciated.

Ms. Raquel D. Bailey provided the assistance in keying and editing a majority of the text. Her diligent effort helped others to move this hobby project forward in the timely fashion. Raquel's Proofing & Editing is acknowledged for providing the secretarial service graciously and in effective and efficient manner.

Our son, Amit A. Shahane and his wife, Alison Mann, are acknowledged for their constant moral support that they have provided without even making the author aware of it.

Finally, acknowledgements are also due to many others who assisted the author directly and indirectly in arriving at this stage of the book.

TABLE OF CONTENTS

Story # Title Page

COMMUNICATION

1. Bubba Applied for an Engineering Position 10
2. Radio Conversation of a US Naval Ship 10
3. Budding Politician 11
4. Early Shopper 12
5. The Salesman and the Homeowner 12

EDUCATIONAL

6. Bible Studies 14
7. Brilliance 14
8. Ten Pretty Good Rules 15
9. The Original Computer 16
10. Riches 16
11. Do the Dogs Like It? 17
12. Blocking the Flow of Inspiration 17
13. I Owe My Mother A Lot 18
14. Stress Management 20
15. A Burning Desire 20
16. Grandmother's Advice 21
17. The Value of a College Education 21
18. A.A.A.D.D. 24
19. Lessons in Life 25
20. Noah's Ark 27
21. Great Advice 27

ENTERTAINING

22. Winston Churchill and the Lady 29
23. What Is 2 + 2 ? 29
24. The Quick Doctor 30
25. A Fly in the Cereal 30
26. School Daze 31
27. The Farmer who Gets a Ticket 31
28. Short Takes 32
29. Calvin Coolidge's Laconic Reply 33

Story #	Title	Page
30	The Mule	33
31	G-Man	34
32	Cowboy	34
33	Southern Lawyers	35
34	Old Farmer's Advice	36
35	The Bathtub	37
36	Can't Top That	37
37	The Phone Connection	38
38	Fifty Dollars	39
39	Let Go!	39
40	Last Wishes	40
41	Scary Ride	40
42	Group Therapy	41
43	Died and Gone to Heaven	41
44	One for You...	42
45	Mad Wife Disease	43
46	Four Brothers	43
47	Coincidences	44
48	Cowboy Sense...	45
49	Getting the Message	46
50	Who is that Idiot?	46
51	Restroom Guidelines	47
52	A Vacation	48
53	Medical Term	48
54	Hillbilly	49
55	Advice for a Long and Blissful Marriage	49
56	Cowboy in Church	50
57	Disconnect	51
58	New Stock Market Terms	52
59	A Tall Order	52

ENVIRONMENT

60	A Paradigm Change for a Family	54
61	Common Knowledge	55
62	Dusting	56
63	Sign of the Times	57

Story #	Title	Page

HISTORICAL

64	An Ohio Woman in the Nineteenth Century	58
65	The Chairman and the Secrets	59
66	Paradigm Changes about the Father in the Lifetime	60
67	Math Progression	61
68	An Oversight by the President of Harvard University	61
69	A Dream	63

HUMAN BEHAVIOR

70	The Man and the Lottery	64
71	A Story of Ray Doss	64
72	Who Thinks He Can	66
73	Divorce vs. Murder	67
74	Points to Ponder	67

INSPIRATIONAL

75	The Classical Letter of a Boy of Six, Written 35 Years Later	69
76	What Is Life?	70
77	George Patton's one Minute Message	71
78	$20.00	71
79	A Word by Rudyard Kipling	72

MISCELLANEOUS

80	A Well Kept Secret in Washington D.C.	73
81	A Cross-Examination	74
82	Thirteen Things that the American High School Graduates have not Learnt in the School	74
83	Leave Statistics	75
84	30 Years Difference!	76
85	What's the Problem?	77
86	Trick Dog	78
87	Things you'd Love to Say at Work, but Can't!	78
88	Grocery List	79
89	The Duck & the Lawyer	80

Story #	Title	Page

MOTIVATIONAL

90	Fleming and Churchill Interactions	82
91	The Pies in Venice, Florida	83
92	Need Help	84
93	I Am a Fortunate Man	84

MYSTERIOUS

94	A Story of the Famous American Singer	86
95	Amy	87
96	Strange Decision Criteria	88
97	Another Strange Decision Criteria	88
98	A Note	89
99	Whose Job is it?	89

PHILOSOPHICAL

100	Feathers in the Wind	91
101	Management 101	91
102	The Cracked Pot	92
103	Why Worry?	93

THOUGHT PROVOKING

104	A Monkey Driving the Car	94
105	A Monkey with the Torch	94
106	The Ship	95
107	Prison vs. Work	96
108	Only in America	96
109	Sins of Omission	97
110	Understanding the 'Stock Market'	97
111	The Explanation of Life	98
112	Conundrum	99
113	Drunken Observations	100
114	Medical Alert	101
115	Man's Best Friend	102

References	103
About the Author	105

COMMUNICATION

Bubba Applied for an Engineering Position - 1

Bubba applied for an engineering position at a Lake Charles refinery. A Yankee applied for the same job and both applicants having the same qualifications were asked to take a test by the manager. Upon completion of the test, both men only missed one of the questions.

The manager went to Bubba and said: "Thank you for your interest but we've decided to give the Yankee the job."

Bubba asked: "And why are you giving him the job? We both got nine questions correct; this being Louisiana, and me being a Southern boy I should get the job!"

The manager said: "We have made our decision not on the correct answers, but rather on the one question that you both missed."

Bubba then asked: "And just how would one incorrect answer be better than the other?" The manager replied: "Bubba, it's like this... on question #4, the Yankee put down, "I don't know." And you put down, "Neither do I."

Source: Reference No. 7

Radio Conversation of a US Naval Ship - 2

Canadians: Please divert your course 15 degrees to the South, to avoid a collision.

Americans: Recommend you divert your course 15 degrees to the North, to avoid a collision.

Canadians: Negative: You will have to divert your course 15 degrees to the South to avoid a collision.

Americans: This is the Captain of a US Navy ship. I say divert YOUR course.

Canadians: Negative. I say again, you will have to divert your course.

Americans: THIS IS THE AIRCRAFT CARRIER USS LINCOLN, THE SEC-

OND LARGEST SHIP IN THE UNITED STATES ATLANTIC FLEET. WE ARE ACCOMPANIED BY THREE DESTROYERS, THREE CRUISERS, AND NUMEROUS SUPPORT VESSELS. I DEMAND THAT YOU CHANGE YOUR COURSE 15 DEGREES NORTH, I SAY AGAIN, THAT'S 15 DEGREES NORTH, OR COUNTERMEASURES WILL BE UNDERTAKEN TO ENSURE THE SAFETY OF THIS SHIP.

Canadians: We are a lighthouse. It's your call.

Source: Reference No. 7

Budding Politician - 3

A young cowboy from Texas goes off to college at Arkansas, but half way through the semester, he has foolishly squandered all his money. He calls home.

"Dad," he says, "You won't believe what modern education is developing! They actually have a program here in Little Rock that will teach your dog, Ol' Blue how to talk!"

"That's amazing," his dad says, "How do I get Ol' Blue in that program?"

"Just send him down here with $1,000," the young cowboy says. "I'll get him in the course."

So his father sends the dog and $1,000.

About two thirds through the semester, the money again runs out. The boy calls home.

"So how's Ol' Blue doing, son," his father asks.

"Awesome, dad, he's talking up a storm," he says, "but you just won't believe this – they've had such good results, they have started to teach the animals how to read!"

"Read!" says the father, "no kidding! How do we get Blue in that program?"

"Just send $2,500, I'll get him in the class."

The money promptly arrives.

But our hero has a problem. At the end of the year, his father will find out the dog can neither talk, nor read. So he shoots the dog.

When he arrives home at the end of the year, his father is all excited.

"Where's Ol' Blue? I just can't wait to see him read something and talk!"

"Dad," the boy says, "I have some bad news. Yesterday morning, just before we left to drive home, Ol' Blue was in the dorm room, kicked back in the bed, reading the Wall Street Journal, like he usually does. Then he turned to me and asked, "So is your daddy still messing around with that little redhead who lives in town?"

The father exclaimed, "I hope you shot that dog before he talks to your mother!"

"I sure did, Dad!"

"That's my boy!"

The kid went on to be a successful lawyer and congressman.

Source: Reference No. 7

Early Shopper - 4

It was Christmas and the judge was in a merry mood as he asked the prisoner, "What are you charged with?"

"Doing my Christmas shopping early," replied the defendant.

"That's no offense," said the judge. "How early were you doing this shopping?"

"Before the store opened," countered the prisoner.

Source: Reference No. 7

The Salesman and the Homeowner - 5

In a small town, a creative salesman noticed that most of the houses were dirty and he wanted to do something about it. He created a vacuum cleaner which cleaned the house completely and with ease.

He started going from house to house to sell his vacuum cleaners. His vacuum cleaners were good and thus he was able to sell the vacuum cleaners to almost every house on the block.

After this success, he visited the next house with an old lady who did not like the salesman coming to her house. She slammed the door on him, but fortunately he was able to stop the closing door with his foot and he entered the house.

He said to the lady that every house in her neighborhood purchased his vacuum cleaner which is the best and it works with ease. He said to the lady that he would spray cow dung on the floor of the house as he had done in every house and if the vacuum cleaner did not pick up the cow dung, he will eat the cow dung himself with a spoon.

The lady immediately replied, "Let me then bring the spoon because you will be eating the cow dung in my house. The city has cut off my electricity for the last two weeks and the house is without electricity."

Source: Anonymous

EDUCATIONAL

Bible Studies - 6

A teenage boy had just passed his motorcycle test and asked his dad if they could discuss his use of the dad's Triumph.

His dad said he'd make a deal with his son. "You bring your 'A' level grades up from a C to a B, study your Bible a little, get your hair cut and we'll talk about the bike."

The teenager thought about that for a moment, decided he'd settle for the offer and they agreed on it.

After about 3 months his father said, "Son, I've been real proud. You brought your grades up and I've observed that you have been studying your Bible, but I'm real disappointed you haven't had your hair cut.

The boy paused a moment then said, "You know, dad, I've been thinking about that, and I've noticed in my studies of the Bible that Samson had long hair, John the Baptist had long hair, Moses had long hair and there's even a strong argument that Jesus had long hair.

To this, his father replied, "Did you also notice that they all walked everywhere they went?"

Source: Reference No. 7

Brilliance - 7

A wealthy old lady decides to go on a photo safari in Africa, taking her faithful aged poodle named "Cuddles" along for the company.

One day the poodle starts chasing butterflies and before long, Cuddles discovers that she's lost. Wandering about, she notices a leopard heading rapidly in her direction with the intention of having lunch.

The old poodle thinks, "Oh, oh! I'm in trouble now!"

Noticing some bones on the ground close by, she immediately settles down to chew on one, her back to the approaching cat. Just as the leopard is about to leap, the old poodle exclaims loudly, "Boy, that was one delicious leopard! I wonder if there are any more around here?"

Hearing this, the young leopard halts his attack in mid-strike, a look of terror coming over him. He slinks away into the trees. "Whew!" says the leopard. "That was close! That old poodle nearly had me!"

Meanwhile, a monkey, who had been watching the whole scene from a nearby tree, figures he can put this knowledge to good use and trade it for protection from the leopard. So off he goes, but the old poodle sees him heading after the leopard with great speed, and figures that something must be up.

The monkey soon catches up with the leopard, spills the beans, and strikes a deal for himself with the leopard.

The young leopard is furious at being made a fool of and says, "Here, monkey, hop on my back and see what's going to happen to that conniving canine!"

Now, the old poodle sees the leopard coming with the monkey on his back and thinks, "What am I going to do now?" but instead of running, the dog sits down with her back to her attackers, pretending she hasn't seen them yet. Just when they get close enough to hear, the old poodle says, "Where's that damned monkey? I sent him off an hour ago to bring me another leopard!"

Source: Reference No. 7

Ten Pretty Good Rules - 8

1. Never wrestle with a pig; you both get dirty, and the pig likes it!
2. Never argue with an idiot; people watching may not be able to tell the difference!
3. Observe everything; admire nothing!
4. It's easier to obtain forgiveness than it is permission!

5. Rarely resist the opportunity to keep your mouth shut!
6. Don't ask questions if you can't live with the answers!
7. If you want a new idea, read an old book!
8. If you don't know where you're going, any road will take you there!
9. Never have a philosophy which supports lack of courage!
10. Never look back unless you intend to go that way!

Source: Reference No. 2

The Original Computer – 9

Memory was something you lost with age
An application was for employment
A program was a TV show
A cursor used profanity
A keyboard was a piano
A web was a spider's home
A virus was the flu
A CD was a bank account
A hard drive was a long trip on the road
A mouse pad was where a mouse lived
And if you had a 3 inch floppy… you just hoped nobody ever found out!

Source: Reference No. 7

Riches - 10

One day a father and his rich family took his son on a trip to the country with the firm purpose to show him how poor people can be. They spent a day and a night in the farm of a very poor family.

When they got back from their trip the father asked his son, "How was the trip?"

"Very good Dad!"

"Did you see how poor people can be?" the father asked.

"Yeah!"

"And what did you learn?"

The son answered, "I saw that we have a dog at home, and they have four. We have a pool that reaches to the middle of the garden, they have a creek that has no end. We have imported lamps in the garden, they have the stars. Our patio reaches to the front yard, they have a whole horizon."

When the little boy was finishing, his father was speechless. His son added, "Thanks Dad for showing me how poor we are!"

Source: Reference No. 7

Do the Dogs Like It? - 11

A sales manager developed a new dog food. All the proteins, minerals, fats, and carbohydrates were included in the product. The company came out with a brand-new package and a national advertising program that included full-page advertisement and ingenious commercials. But after six months, the sales (which had started slowly) had finally dwindled to nothing. So the chairman of the board called all the district sales managers together in a major convention in Chicago. "What's wrong?" he asked. "Look at the beautiful full-page advertisement we have in national magazines. Look at the expensive commercials on television." Then he held up a box of the dog food and pointed to the back of the box. He read the contents and admired the beautiful packaging. "The cost is even lower than our competitors," he added. "Now tell me why you people aren't selling this dog food!" You would hear a pin drop silence. Then someone in the back of the room slowly came to his feet and said, "Sir, the dogs don't like it!"

Source: Reference No. 11

Blocking the Flow of Inspiration - 12

This story is about Leonardo da Vinci. According to the legend, some children were visiting the famous artist. One of them knocked over a stack of canvases. This upset the artist because he was working very quietly and sensitively. He became angry, threw his brush, and hurled some harsh words to the helpless little fellow who ran crying from the studio.

The artist was now alone again, and he tried to continue his work. He was trying to paint the face of Jesus, but he couldn't do it. His creativity had stopped.Leonardo da Vinci put down his brush. He went out and walked to the streets and the alleys until he found the little boy. He said, "I'm sorry, son; I shouldn't have spoken so harshly. Forgive me. I have done something worse than you. You only knocked over the canvases. But I, by my anger, blocked the flow of God into my life. Will you come back with me?"He took the boy back into the studio with him. They smiled as the face of Jesus came quite naturally from the master's brush. That face has been an inspiration to millions ever since.

Source: Reference No. 12

I Owe My Mother A Lot - 13

My mother taught me to appreciate a job well done. "If you're going to kill each other, do it outside. I just finished cleaning."

My mother taught me religion: "You better pray that will come out of the carpet."

My mother taught me about time travel. "If you don't straighten up, I'm going to knock you into the middle of next week!"

My mother taught me logic. "Because I said so, that's why."

My mother taught me more logic. "If you fall out of that swing and break your neck, you're not going to the store with me."

My mother taught me foresight... "Make sure you wear clean underwear, in case you're in an accident."

My mother taught me irony... "Keep crying and I'll give you something to cry about."

My mother taught me about the science of osmosis...

"Shut your mouth and eat your supper!"

My mother taught me about contortionism... "Will you look at the dirt on the back of your neck!"

My mother taught me about stamina... "You'll sit there 'till all that spinach is finished."

My mother taught me about weather... "It looks as if a tornado swept through your room."

My mother taught me about hypocrisy. "If I told you once, I've told you a million times. Don't exaggerate!"

My mother taught me the circle of life. "I brought you into this world, and I can take you out."

My mother taught me about behavior modification. "Stop acting like your father!"

My mother taught me about envy. "There are millions of less fortunate children in this world who don't have wonderful parents like you do."

My mother taught me about anticipation. "Just wait until we get home."

My mother taught me about receiving. "You are going to get it when you get home!"

My mother taught me medical science. "If you don't stop crossing your eyes, they are going to get stuck that way."

My mother taught me ESP. "Put your sweater on; don't you think I know when you are cold?"

My mother taught me humor. "When that lawn mower cuts off your toes, don't come running to me."

My mother taught me how to become an adult. "If you don't eat your vegetables, you'll never grow up."

My mother taught me genetics. "You're just like your father."

My mother taught me about my roots. "Shut that door behind you. Do you think you were born in a barn?"

My mother taught me wisdom. "When you get to be my age, you'll understand."

And my favorite: My mother taught me about justice. "One day you'll have kids, and I hope they turn out just like you.

Source: Reference No. 7

Stress Management - 14

A lecturer, when explaining stress management to an audience, raised a glass of water and asked, "How much does this glass of water weigh?" Answers called out ranged from 20g to 500g.

The lecturer replied, "The absolute weight doesn't matter. It depends on how long you try to hold it. If I hold it for a minute, that's not a problem. If I hold it for an hour, I'll have an ache in my arm. If I hold it for a day, you'd have to call an ambulance."

"In each case, it's the same weight, but the longer I hold it, the heavier it becomes." He continued, "And that's the way it is with stress management. If we carry our burdens all the time, sooner or later, as the burden becomes increasingly heavy, we won't be able to carry on."

"As with the glass of water, you have to put it down for a while and rest before holding it again. When we're refreshed, we can carry on with the burden."

"So, before you return home tonight, put down the burden of work. Don't carry it home. You can pick it up tomorrow. Whatever burdens you're carrying now, let them down for a moment if you can. Relax; pick them up later after you've rested. Life is short. Enjoy it!"

Source: Reference No. 7

A Burning Desire - 15

A story is told of a young man who approached the great philosopher Socrates, and said, "Master, teach me all that you know. I want to know all that you know."

Socrates agreed and asked this young man to walk with him. They were walking on a road with a shallow lake. Socrates asked the young man to walk into shallow water. They continued to walk into the water. It rose to their ankles, then knees, then hips, until they were standing in water up to their shoulders. Socrates put his arm around the young man's shoulders and tightened around the young man's neck and pulled him underneath the water. During the first 15-20 seconds, the young man had inhaled enough air to be in no danger. At 30 seconds the young man wondered whether Socrates was going to let him up. He began to give an indication to Socrates that it was too long. A few seconds later, the young man began to fight with all his strength. He clawed and scratched but the hold was too strong and he lost his strength. At that moment, Socrates pulled him out of the water, dragged him to the shore, and began to revive him.

Angry and confused, the young man caught his breath and asked, "Socrates, what was that all about?" Socrates looked into his eyes and said, "When you want to know what I know as much as you just wanted to live, then you will know." That kind of desire is known as a burning desire!"

Source: Reference No. 15

A Grandmother's Advice - 16

In the wonderful memoir What We Do for Love, author Ilene Beckerman ends the book with this advice from her grandmother:

"If you have to stand on your head to make somebody happy, all you can expect is a big headache."

Source: Reference No. 1

The Value of a College Education - 17

Many of you young persons out there are seriously thinking about going to college. (That is, of course, a lie. The only things you young persons think seriously about are beer, loud music and sex. Trust me: these are closely related to college.)

Basically, you learn two kinds of things in college:

Things you will need to know in later life (two hours). These include how to make collect phone calls and get beer and crepe-paper stains out of your pajamas.

Things you will not need to know in later life (1,998 hours). These are the things you learn in classes whose names end in -ology, - -osophy, -istry, -ics, and so on. The idea is, you memorize these things, then write them down in little exam books, then forget them. If you fail to forget them, you become a professor and have to stay in college for the rest of your life.

It's very difficult to forget everything. For example, when I was in college, I had to memorize — don't ask me why — the names of three metaphysical poets other than John Donne. I have managed to forget one of them, but I still remember that the other two were named Vaughan and Crashaw. Sometimes, when I'm trying to remember something important like whether my wife told me to get tuna packed in oil or tuna packed in water, Vaughan and Crashaw just pop up in my mind, right there in the supermarket. It's a terrible waste of brain cells.

After you've been in college for a year or so, you're supposed to choose a major, which is the subject you intend to memorize and forget the most things about. Here is a very important piece of advice: Be sure to choose a major that does not involve Known Facts and Right Answers. This means you must *not* major in mathematics, physics, biology, or chemistry, because these subjects involve actual facts. If, for example, you major in mathematics, you're going to wander into class one day and the professor will say: "Define the cosine integer of the quadrant of a rhomboid binary axis, and extrapolate your result to five significant vertices." If you don't come up with exactly the answer the professor has in mind, you fail. The same is true of chemistry: if you write in your exam book that carbon and hydrogen combine to form oak, your professor will flunk you. He wants you to come up with the same answer he and all the other chemists have agreed on. Scientists are extremely snotty about this.

So you should major in subjects like English, philosophy, psychology, and sociology — subjects in which nobody really understands what anybody else is talking about, and which involve virtually no actual facts. I attended classes in all these subjects, so I'll give you a quick overview of each:

ENGLISH: This involves writing papers about long books you have read little snippets of just before class. Here is a tip on how to get good grades on your English papers: Never say anything about a book that anybody with any common sense would say. For example, suppose you are studying Moby-Dick. Anybody with any common sense would say that Moby-Dick is a big white whale, since the characters in the book refer to it as a big white whale roughly eleven thousand times. So in your paper, you say Moby-Dick is actually the Republic of Ireland. Your professor, who is sick to death of reading papers and never liked Moby-Dick anyway, will think you are enormously creative. If you can regularly come up with lunatic interpretations of simple stories, you should major in English.

PHILOSOPHY: Basically, this involves sitting in a room and deciding there is no such thing as reality and then going to lunch. You should major in philosophy if you plan to take a lot of drugs.

PSYCHOLOGY: This involves talking about rats and dreams. Psychologists are obsessed with rats and dreams. I once spent an entire semester training a rat to punch little buttons in a certain sequence, then training my roommate to do the same thing. The rat learned much faster. My roommate is now a doctor. If you like rats or dreams, and above all if you dream about rats, you should major in psychology.

SOCIOLOGY: For sheer lack of intelligibility, sociology is far and away the number one subject. I sat through hundreds of hours of sociology courses, and read gobs of sociology writing, and I never once heard or read a coherent statement. This is because sociologists want to be considered scientists, so they spend most of their time translating simple, obvious observations into scientific-sounding code. If you plan to major in sociology, you'll have to learn to do the same thing. For example, suppose you have observed that children cry when they fall down. You should write: "Methodological observation of the sociometrical behavior tendencies of prematurated isolates indicates that a causal relationship exists between groundward tropism and lachrimatory, or 'crying,' behavior forms." If you can keep this up for fifty or sixty pages, you will get large government grants.

Source: Reference No. 4

A.A.A.D.D - 18

Recently, I was diagnosed with A.A.A.D.D. Age Activated Attention Deficit Disorder. This is how it manifests:

I decide to wash my car.

As I start toward the garage, I notice that there is mail on the hall table. I decide to go through the mail before I wash the car. I lay my car keys down on the table, put the junk mail in the trash can under the table, and notice that the trash can is full. So, I decide to put the bills back on the table and take out the trash first.

But then I think, since I'm going to be near the mailbox when I take out the trash anyway, I may as well pay the bills first. I take my checkbook off the table, and see that there is only one check left. My extra checks are in my desk in the study, so I go to my desk where I find the can of Coke that I had been drinking.

I'm going to look for my checks, but first I need to push the Coke aside so that I don't accidentally knock it over. I see that the Coke is getting warm, and I decide I should put it in the refrigerator to keep it cold. As I head toward the kitchen with the coke a vase of flowers on the counter catches my eye— they need to be watered. I set the Coke down on the counter, and I discover my reading glasses that I've been searching for all morning.

I decide I better put them back on my desk, but first I'm going to water the flowers. I set the glasses back down on the counter, fill a container with water and suddenly I spot the TV remote. Someone left it on the kitchen table. I realize that tonight when we go to watch TV, I will be looking for the remote, but I won't remember that it's on the kitchen table, so

I decide to put it back in the den where it belongs, but first I'll water the flowers.

I splash some water on the flowers, but most of it spills on the floor. So, I set the remote back down on the table, get some towels and wipe up the spill. Then I head down the hall trying to remember what I was planning to do.

At the end of the day: the car isn't washed, the bills aren't paid, there is a warm can of Coke sitting on the counter, the flowers aren't watered, there is still only one check in my checkbook, I can't find the remote, I can't find my glasses, and I don't remember what I did with the car keys.

Then when I try to figure out why nothing got done today, I'm really baffled because I know I was busy all day long, and I'm really tired. I realize this is a serious problem, and I'll try to get some help for it, but first I'll check my e-mail. Do me a favor, will you? Forward this message to everyone you know, because I don't remember to whom it has been sent.

Don't laugh – if this isn't you yet, your day is coming!

Source: Anonymous

Lessons in Life - 19

Life isn't fair, but it's still good.
When in doubt, just take the next small step.
Life is too short to waste time hating anyone.
Don't take yourself so seriously. No one else does.
Pay off your credit cards every month.
You don't have to win every argument. Agree to disagree.
Cry with someone. It's more healing than crying alone.
It's OK to get angry with God. He can take it.
Save for retirement starting with your first paycheck.
When it comes to chocolate, resistance is futile.
Make peace with your past so it doesn't screw up the present.
It's okay to let your children see you cry.
Don't compare your life to others'. You have no idea what their

journey is all about.

If a relationship has to be a secret, you shouldn't be in it.

Everything can change in the blink of an eye. But don't worry; God never blinks.

Life is too short for long pity parties. Get busy living, or get busy dying.

You can get through anything if you stay put in today.

A writer writes. If you want to be a writer, write.

It's never too late to have a happy childhood. But the second one is up to you and no one else.

When it comes to going after what you love in life, don't take no for an answer.

Burn the candles, use the nice sheets, wear the fancy lingerie. Don't save it for a special occasion. Today is special.

Over prepare, and then go with the flow.

Be eccentric now. Don't wait for old age to wear purple.

The most important sex organ is the brain.

No one is in charge of your happiness except you.

Frame every so-called disaster with these words: "In five years, will this matter?"

Always choose life.

Forgive everyone everything.

What other people think of you is none of your business.

Time heals almost everything. Give time time.

However good or bad a situation is, it will change.

Your job won't take care of you when you are sick. Your friends will. Stay in touch.

Believe in miracles.

God loves you because of who God is, not because of anything you did or didn't do.

Whatever doesn't kill you really does make you stronger.

Growing old beats the alternative — dying young.

Read the Psalms. They cover every human emotion.

Get outside every day. Miracles are waiting everywhere.

If we all threw our problems in a pile and saw everyone else's, we'd grab ours back.

Don't audit life. Show up and make the most of it now.

Get rid of anything that isn't useful, beautiful or joyful.
All that truly matters in the end is that you loved.
Envy is a waste of time. You already have all you need.
The best is yet to come.
No matter how you feel, get up, dress up and show up.
Take a deep breath. It calms the mind.
If you don't ask, you don't get.
Yield.
Life isn't tied with a bow, but it's still a gift.

Source: Reference No. 7

Noah's Ark - 20

1. Don't miss the boat….
2. Remember that we are all in the same boat.
3. Plan ahead. It wasn't raining when Noah built the Ark.
4. Stay fit When you're 600 years old, someone may ask you to do something really big.
5. Don't listen to critics; just get on with the job that needs to be done.
6. Build your future on high ground.
7. For safety's sake, travel in pairs.
8. Speed isn't always an advantage. The snails were on board with the cheetahs.
9. When you're stressed, float a while.
10. Remember, the Ark was built by amateurs; the Titanic by professionals.
11. No matter the storm, when you are with God, there's always a rainbow waiting…

Source: Reference No. 7

Great Advice - 21

Once there was a politician who did the best job he could. But being human, he made mistakes and was criticized, and reporters repeated errors of fact about him in the paper. Well, he became so upset that he drove out into the country to visit his dear friend, a farmer.

"What am I going to do?" the politician cried. "I've tried so hard. Nobody has tried harder than I have to do more good for more people – and look how they criticize me.But the farmer could hardly hear the complaint of his persecuted politician friend because his hound dog was barking at the full moon. The farmer rebuked his dog, but the dog kept barking. Finally the farmer said to the politician, "Do you want to know how you should handle your unfair critics? Here's how. Listen to that dog. Now, look at the moon. And remember that people will keep yelling at you – they'll nip at your heels, and they'll criticize you. But here's the lesson: the dog keeps howling, but the moon keeps shining!"

Let people persecute you – but don't stop doing all the good you've been doing.

Source: Reference No. 12

ENTERTAINING

Winston Churchill and the Lady - 22

One day Mr. Winston Churchill, the Prime Minister of Great Britain during the World War II, was Strolling in London. He entered into a coffee-shop and bought a cup of coffee and sat down. The lady sitting on the other side of the table said to him, "I know who you are! You are Mr. Churchill."

While that was pleasing to Mr. Churchill, she continued, and said "Mr. Churchill, I want to tell you that I don't like you as a Prime Minister and I don't even like your face. I hate your guts." That caught Mr. Churchill by surprise. But, the woman continued and said "Mr. Churchill, if I was your wife, I would put poison in your coffee".

Mr. Churchill looked straight into her eyes and said, "Madam, if you were my wife, I would drink that coffee with poison in it"

Source: Anonymous

What Is 2 + 2 ? - 23

There was a company that was in the process of selecting its President. There were three applicants – a CPA, and engineer and a full-time Professional Toastmaster. Although they have different backgrounds, they have identical stages of experience. The research committee got confused. Finally, the committee decided to ask this question, "What is 2 + 2?". The CPA said, it is 4 because if you give me 2 dollars and again 2 dollars, it will be four dollars. The engineer said that 2 + 2 is not necessarily four, in most systems it is four, but not always. When a toastmaster was asked that question, the reply was, "2 + 2 is what you like it to be! You want 7? The answer is 7. You want 5? The answer is five.

Source: Reference No. 14

The Quick Doctor - 24

Three professional doctors (a psychologist, a psychiatrist and a surgeon) gathered around a lake. Each of them was given a shotgun. A flock of birds was to fly from one end of the lake and was to pass over the lake right in front of their eyes. Their job was to shoot down as many ducks as possible from that flock of birds.

As the flock came in, the psychologist recognized the first bird as the bald eagle and by the time he gets a chance to evaluate the next bird, the flock disappeared at the end of the lake.

The psychiatrist was very amazed to see that the first bird was a turkey, but in his moments of amusement, he lost the flock. Like the psychologist, he did not shoot any bird let alone the duck.

As soon as the surgeon saw the flock, he started the shotgun and fired it several times and shot several birds. He then turned to his assistant, and said "Now you make sure that they all are ducks!"

Source: Anonymous

A Fly in the Cereal - 25

Three friends, an Italian, a Catholic and a Scottish, ordered cereal for breakfast.

After receiving the cereal with milk, an Italian saw a fly in the cereal. He pointed it out to a waitress and ordered her to take it back and bring another bowl of cereal.

When Catholic saw the fly in his cereal, he determined that it was small. He removed it with his spoon and started eating the cereal as if nothing happened.

When Scottish saw the fly in his cereal, he grabbed the fly

and said to the fly "Spit it out now". He then let the fly go and started on his breakfast.

Source: Reference No. 13

School Daze - 26

A Sunday school teacher was testing the children in her Sunday school class to see if they understood the concept of getting to heaven.

She asked them, "If I sold my house and my car, had a big garage sale and gave all my money to the church, would that get me into heaven?"

"No!" the children answered."If I cleaned the church every day, mowed the yard, would that get me into heaven?" Again the answer was, "No!"

Well, then, if I was kind to animals and gave candy to all the children, and loved my husband, would that get me into heaven?" She asked them again. Again, they all answered, "No!"

"Well", she continued, "then how can I get into heaven?"

A five year old boy shouted out, "YOU GOTTA BE DEAD."

Source: Reference No. 7

The Farmer who Gets a Ticket - 27

A farmer got pulled over by a state trooper for speeding, and the trooper started to lecture the farmer about his speed, and in general began to throw his weight around to try to make the farmer uncomfortable. Finally, the trooper got around to writing out the ticket, and as he was doing that he kept swatting at some flies that were buzzing around his head. The farmer said, "Having some problems with circle flies there, are ya?"

The trooper stopped writing the ticket and said—"Well yeah, if that's what they are—I never heard of circle flies". So the farmer says—"Well, circle flies are common on farms. See, they're called circle flies because they're almost always found circling around the back end of a horse."

The trooper says, "Oh," and goes back to writing the ticket.

Then after a minute he stops and says, "Hey...wait a minute, are you trying to call me a horse's behind?"

The farmer says, "Oh no, officer. I have too much respect for law enforcement and police officers to even think about calling you a horse's behind."

The trooper says, "Well, that's a good thing," and goes back to writing the ticket.

After a long pause, the farmer says, "Hard to fool them flies though."

Source: Reference No. 7

Short Takes - 28

A Sign posted on the wall of an Army mess read:
"Don't Waste Food – Food will win the war."
Beneath, someone had written:
"That's fine, but how do we get the enemy to eat it?"

Kirk Douglas Story:

Mr. Douglas Kirk, an American Actor, is married for 60 years. When he got married, he told his wife that now he got married to her and since he loved her tremendously, his wife should serve him a breakfast everyday in bed. His wife snapped back and said, "Kirk, since I love you, I will be happy to serve you with daily breakfast in bed, but then you have to sleep every day in the kitchen."

Bob Hope's Last Words:

Mr. Bob Hope was an icon for humor for a full century (1905 – 2005). In 2005 when Bob Hope was in poor health and when he was at the end of his life on this planet earth, his son asked Bob Hope, "Daddy, what kind of casket do you want?" Bob

Hope replied, "Son, surprise me please!"
Source: Reference No. 7 & 13

Calvin Coolidge's Laconic Reply - 29

Calvin Coolidge was known to be a man of few words, so much so that his nickname was "Silent Cal".

At one dinner he attended, a young lady seated near him indicated to the President that prior to the event she had made a bet with her friends that she could get the President to speak at least three words.

His reply...."You lose!"
Source: Reference No. 3

The Mule - 30

An old Alabama farmer had a wife who nagged him unmercifully. From morning till night (and sometimes later), she was always complaining about something. The only time he got any relief was when he was out plowing with his old mule. He tried to plow a lot.

One day, when he was out plowing, his wife brought him lunch in the field. He drove the old mule into the shade, sat down on a stump and began to eat his lunch. Immediately, his wife began haranguing him again. Complain, nag, nag; it just went on and on.

All of a sudden the old mule lashed out with both hind feet, caught her smack in the back of the head and killed her dead on the spot.

At the funeral several days later, the minister noticed something rather odd. When a woman mourner would approach the old farmer, he would listen for a minute, then nod his head in agreement. This was so consistent, the minister decided to ask the old farmer about it.

So after the funeral, the minister spoke to the old farmer, and asked him why he nodded his head and agreed with the women, but always shook his head and disagreed with all the men.

The old farmer said: "Well, the women would come up and say something about how nice my wife looked, or how pretty her dress was, so I'd nod my head in agreement."

"And what about the men?" the minister asked. They wanted to know if the mule was for sale."

Source: Reference No. 7

G-Man - 31

A Department of Agriculture representative stopped at a farm and said to the old farmer, "I'm here to inspect your farm."

The old farmer said, "You'd better not go out in that field."

The Agriculture representative said in a demanding tone, "I have the authority of the U.S. Government behind me. See this card, I am allowed to go wherever I wish on agricultural land."

So the old farmer went about his chores. In a few minutes, he heard loud screams and saw the Department of Agriculture representative running for his life, headed for the fence. Close behind, and gaining with every step, was the farmer's prize bull, nostrils flaring, madder than a full nest of hornets.

The old farmer cupped his hands to his mouth and yelled out. "Show him your card! Show him your card!"

Source: Reference No. 7

Cowboy - 32

A cowboy went to an insurance agency to buy a policy. The agent asked, "Have you ever had an accident?"

"Nope," replied the cowboy. "Last summer, a bronc kicked in two of my ribs, and a couple of years ago, a rattlesnake bit me on the ankle."

"Wouldn't you call those accidents?" quizzed the puzzled agent.

"Naw," the cowboy replied. "They did it on purpose!"
Source: Reference No. 7

Southern Lawyers - 33

Lawyers should never ask a witness a question if they aren't prepared for the answer.

In a trial, a Southern small town prosecuting attorney called his first witness, a grandmotherly elderly woman to the stand.

He approached her and asked, "Mrs.. Jones, do you know me?"

She responded, "Why, yes, I do know you, Mr. Williams. I've known you since you were a young boy, and frankly, you've been a big disappointment to me. You lie, cheat on your wife, manipulate people and talk about them behind their backs. You think you're a big shot when you haven't the brains to realize you never will amount to anything more than a two-bit paper pusher. Yes, I know you."

The lawyer was stunned! Not knowing what else to do, he pointed across the room and asked, "Mrs.. Jones, do you know the defense attorney?"

She again replied, "Why, yes, I do. I've known Mr. Bradley since he was a youngster too. He's lazy, bigoted, and he has a drinking problem. He can't build a normal relationship with anyone and his law practice is one of the worst in the entire state. Not to mention he cheated on his wife with three different women. One of them was your wife. Yes I know him."

The defense attorney almost died.

The judge asked both lawyers to approach the bench and in a quiet voice, said, "If either of you scoundrels asks her if she knows me, I'll jail you for contempt."

Source: Reference No. 7

Old Farmer's Advice – 34

Your fences need to be horse-high, pig-tight and bull-strong.

Keep skunks and bankers and lawyers at a distance.

Life is simpler when you plow around the stump.

A bumblebee is considerably faster than a John Deere tractor.

Words that soak into your ears are whispered…not yelled.

Meanness don't jes' happen overnight.

Forgive your enemies. It messes up their heads.

Do not corner something that you know is meaner than you.

It don't take a very big person to carry a grudge.

You cannot unsay a cruel word.

Every path has a few puddles.

When you wallow with pigs, expect to get dirty.

The best sermons are lived, not preached.

Most of the stuff people worry about ain't never gonna happen, anyway.

Don't judge folks by their relatives.

Remember that silence is sometimes the best answer.

Live a good, honorable life. Then when you get older and think back, you'll enjoy it a second time.

Don't interfere with something that ain't botherin' you none.

Timing has a lot to do with the outcome of a rain dance.

If you find yourself in a hole, the first thing to do is stop diggin'.

Sometimes you get, and sometimes you get got.

The biggest troublemaker you'll probably ever have to deal with watches you from the mirror every mornin'.

Always drink upstream from the herd.

Good judgment comes from experience, and a lotta that comes from bad judgment.

Lettin' the cat outta the bag is a whole lot easier than puttin' it back.

If you get to thinkin' you're a person of some influence, try orderin' somebody else's dog around.

Live simply. Love generously. Care deeply. Speak kindly. Leave the rest to God…

Source: Reference No. 7

The Bathtub - 35

During a visit to the mental asylum, a visitor asked the Director what the criterion was which defined whether or not a patient should be institutionalized.

"Well," said the Director, "we fill up a bathtub, then we offer a teaspoon, a teacup and a bucket to the patient and ask him or her to empty the bathtub."

"Oh, I understand," said the visitor. "A normal person would use the bucket because it's bigger than the spoon or the teacup."

"No." said the Director, "A normal person would pull the plug. Do you want a bed near the window?"

Source: Reference No. 7

Can't Top That - 36

A Georgia State Trooper pulled a car over on I-95 about 2 miles south of the Georgia/South Carolina state line. When the Trooper asked the driver why he was speeding, the driver answered that he was a magician and a juggler and he was on his way to Savannah to do a show that night at the Shrine Circus and didn't want to be late.

The Trooper told the driver he was fascinated by juggling, and if the driver would do a little juggling for him then he wouldn't give him a ticket.

The driver told the Trooper that he had sent all of his equipment on ahead and didn't have anything to juggle.

The Trooper told him that he had some flares in the trunk of his patrol car and asked if he could juggle them.

The juggler stated that he could, so the Trooper got three flares, lit them and handed them to the juggler.

While the man was doing his juggling act, a car pulled in behind the patrol car. A drunk, good old boy, from S.C., got out and watched the performance briefly He then went over to the patrol car, opened the rear door and got in.

The Trooper observed him doing this and went over to the patrol car, opened the door and asked the drunk what he thought he was doing.

The drunk replied, "You might as well take my ass to jail, because there's no way in hell I can pass that test."

Source: Reference No. 7

The Phone Connection - 37

An Indiana farm wife called the local phone company to report her telephone failed to ring when her friends called, and that on the few occasions when it did ring, her pet dog always moaned right before the phone rang.

The telephone repairman proceeded to the scene, curious to see this psychic dog or senile elderly lady. He climbed a nearby telephone pole, hooked in his test set, and dialed the subscriber's house. The phone didn't ring right away, but then the dog moaned loudly and the telephone began to ring. Climbing down from the pole, the telephone repairman found:
1. The dog was tied to the telephone system's ground wire via a steel chain and collar.
2. The wire connection to the ground rod was loose.
3. The dog was receiving 90 volts of signaling current when the phone number was called.
4. After a couple of such jolts, the dog would start moaning and then urinate on himself and the ground.
5. The wet ground would complete the circuit, thus causing the phone to ring.

Source: Reference No. 7

Fifty Dollars - 38

Farmer John and his wife Ruth went to the state fair every year, and every year John would say, "Ruth, I'd like to ride in that helicopter."

Ruth always replied, "I know John, but that helicopter ride is 50 dollars and 50 dollars is 50 dollars."

One year Ruth and John went to the fair and John said, "Ruth, I'm 85 years old. If I don't ride that helicopter, I might never get another chance." Ruth replied, "John that helicopter is 50 dollars and 50 dollars is 50 dollars." The pilot overheard the couple and said, "Folks, I'll make you a deal. I'll take both of you for a ride. If you can stay quiet for the entire ride and not say a word, I won't charge you a dime! But if you say one word, it's 50 dollars." John and Ruth agreed and up they went. The pilot did all kinds of fancy maneuvers, but not a word was heard. He did his dare devil tricks over and over again, but still not a word.

When they landed, the pilot turned to John and said, "By golly, I did everything I could to get you to yell out, but you didn't. I'm impressed!"

John replied, "Well I almost said something when Ruthie fell out, but you know, 50 dollars is 50 dollars!

Source: Reference No. 7

Let Go! - 39

Eleven people hanging on a rope from a helicopter... they were being rescued, ten men and one woman. Well, the rope couldn't sustain them all; it was destined to break, and they would all die, so one of them had to let go. The woman looked at the ten men, all hanging on for dear life, and she said, "Relax, I'm going to let go because all my life I've given up things for men. All my life I had to make the sacrifices and I never got any thanks. I'm used to it. So I'll let go." And, with that, all ten men applauded!

Source: Reference No. 11

Last Wishes – 40

Mary Clancy goes up to Father O'Grady after his Sunday morning service and she's in tears. He says, "So what's bothering you, Mary my dear?"

She says, "Oh, Father, I've got terrible news. My husband passed away last night."

The priest says, "Oh, Mary, that's terrible. Tell me, Mary, did he have any last requests?"

She says, "That he did, Father..."

The priest says, "What did he ask, Mary?"

She says, "He said, 'Please Mary, put down that damn gun...'

Source: Reference No. 7

Scary Ride - 41

A plane was taking off from Kennedy Airport. After it reached a comfortable cruising altitude, the captain made an announcement over the intercom.

"Ladies and gentlemen, this is your captain speaking. Welcome to Flight 293, nonstop from New York to Los Angeles. The weather ahead is good and therefore we should have a smooth and uneventful flight. Now, please sit back and relax – OH MY GOD!"

Silence. Then, the captain came back on the intercom and said,

"Ladies and gentlemen, I am so sorry if I scared you earlier, but while I was talking, the flight attendant brought me a cup of coffee and spilled the hot coffee in my lap. You should see the front of my pants!"

A passenger in coach piped up, "That's nothing. You should see the back of mine!"

Source: Reference No. 7

Group Therapy - 42

Clergymen spend a lot of time consoling and consoling others, but have little outlet for their own problems. Thus, the heads of the various churches in a small town decided to get together for a sort of group therapy session. They met in a park outside of town and began to talk.

The first minister said, "My allowance is rather meager, and I have to admit that sometimes I will skim a little money from the collection plate for myself." The others agreed that a man has to live comfortably and that this sounds fine, as long as he doesn't get extravagant.

The second minister said, "I am in charge of the wine cellar for communion, and sometimes after a hard day, I'll go down and have a few glasses of wine." The others don't see any harm in this, as long as he doesn't get stinking drunk.

The next to speak said, "Sometimes I fantasize about the young women in the congregation." This is similarly accepted and counseled.

Finally, they turn to the last minister, who hasn't said anything. "What do you wish to talk about?" The minister just shakes his head and says "No, no, it's all right. I'm ok." The others work on him, saying that everyone has problems, it's ok to talk about them, they're all peers, etc.

Finally the minister flushes strongly, looks at the ground, and says, "Well, you see, ... I'm a terrible gossip, and I can't wait to get back to town!"

Source: Reference No. 7

Died and Gone to Heaven - 43

Three buddies died in a car crash and when they got to heaven they attended orientation. They were all asked, "When you are in your casket and your family and friends are mourning your loss, what would you like to hear them say about you?"

The first guy replied, "I'd like to hear them say that I was a great doctor of my time and a great family man."

The second guy said, "I'd like to hear that I was a wonderful husband and school teacher who made a huge difference in the lives of children."

And the third guy replied, "I'd like to hear them say, 'Look, he's moving!"

Source: Reference No. 7

One for You... - 44

On the outskirts of a small town, there was a big, old pecan tree just inside the cemetery fence. One day, two boys filled up a bucketful of nuts and sat down by the tree, out of sight, and began dividing the nuts.

"One for you, one for me. One for you, one for me," said one boy. Several dropped and rolled down toward the fence.

Another boy came riding along the road on his bicycle. As he passed, he thought he heard voices from inside the cemetery. He slowed down to investigate. Sure enough, he heard, "One for you, one for me. One for you, one for me."

He just knew what it was. He jumped back on his bike and rode off. Just around the bend he met an old man with a cane, hobbling along.

"Come here quick," said the boy, "you won't believe what I heard!

Satan and the Lord are down at the cemetery dividing up the souls."

The man said, "Beat it kid, can't you see it's hard for me to walk."

When the boy insisted though, the man hobbled slowly to the cemetery. Standing by the fence they heard, "One for you, one for me. One for you, one for me..."

The old man whispered, "Boy, you've been tellin' me the truth. Let's see if we can see the Lord." Shaking with fear, they peered through the fence, yet were still unable to see anything.

The old man and the boy gripped the wrought iron bars of the fence tighter and tighter as they tried to get a glimpse of the Lord. At last they heard, "One for you, one for me. That's all. Now let's go get those nuts by the fence and we'll be done."

They say the old man made it back to town a full 5 minutes ahead of the kid on the bike.

Source: Reference No. 7

Mad Wife Disease - 45

A guy was sitting quietly reading his paper when his wife walked up behind him and whacked him on the head with a magazine. "What was that for?" he asked.

"That was for the piece of paper in your pants pocket with the name Laura Lou written on it," she replied.

"Two weeks ago when I went to the races, Laura Lou was the name of one of the horses I bet on," he explained.

"Oh honey, I'm sorry," she said. "I should have known there was a good explanation." Three days later he was watching a ball game on TV when she walked up and hit him on the head again, this time with the iron skillet, which knocked him out cold. When he came to, he asked, "What was that for?"

She replied... "Your horse called."

Source: Reference No. 7

Four Brothers - 46

Four brothers left home for college, and they became successful doctors and lawyers and prospered.

Some years later, they chatted after having dinner together. They discussed the gifts they were able to give their elderly mother who lived far away in another city.

The first said, "I had a big house built for Mama."

The second said, "I had a hundred thousand dollar theater built in the house."

The third said, "I had my Mercedes dealer deliver an SL600 to her."

The fourth said, "You know how Mamma loved reading the Bible and you know she can't read anymore because she can't see very well. I met this preacher who told me about a parrot that can recite the entire bible. It took twenty preachers 12 years to teach him. I had to pledge to contribute $100,000 a year for twenty years to the church, but it was worth it. Mamma just has to name the chapter and verse and the parrot will recite it."

The other brothers were impressed.

After the holidays Mom sent out her Thank You notes. She wrote:

"Milton, the house you built is so huge I live in only one room, but I have to clean the whole house. Thanks anyway."

"Marvin, I am too old to travel. I stay home; I have my groceries delivered, so I never use the Mercedes. The thought was good. Thanks."

"Michael, you gave me an expensive theater with Dolby sound, it could hold 50 people, but all of my friends are dead, I've lost my hearing, and I'm nearly blind. I'll never use it. Thank you for the gesture just the same."

"Dearest Melvin, you were the only son to have the good sense to give a little thought to your gift. The chicken was delicious. Thank you."

Source: Reference No. 7

Coincidences - 47

Two men were sitting next to each other at a bar. After awhile, one guy looks at the other and says, "I can't help but think, from listening to you, that you're from Ireland."

The other guy responds proudly, "Yes, that I am!"

The first guy says, "So am I! And where about from Ireland might you be?"

The other guy answers, "I'm from Dublin, I am."

The first guy responds, "Sure and begora, and so am I. And what street did you live on in Dublin?"

The other guy says, "A lovely little area it was. I lived on McCleary Street in the old central part of town." The first guy says, "Faith and it's a small world. So did I! And to what school would you have been going?"

The other guy answers, "Well now, I went to St. Mary's, of course."

The first guy gets really excited and says, "And so did I. Tell me, what year did you graduate?"

The other guy answers, "Well, now, let's see. I graduated in 1964."

The first guy exclaims, "The Good Lord must be smiling down upon us! I can hardly believe our good luck at winding up in the same bar tonight. Can you believe it? I graduated from St. Mary's in 1964 my own self!"

The bartender walks over, shaking his head and mutters, "It's going to be a long night tonight. The Murphy twins are drunk again."

Source: Reference No. 7

Cowboy Sense... - 48

There is no arguing with cowboy logic. The Sierra Club and the United States Forest Service (USFS) were presenting an alternative to Wyoming ranchers for controlling the coyote population. It seems that after years of the ranchers using the tried and true methods of shooting and/or trapping the predator, the tree-huggers had a "more humane" solution. What they proposed was for the animals to be captured alive, the males castrated and let loose again and the population would be controlled.

This was actually proposed to the Wyoming Wool and Sheep Grower's Association by the Sierra Club and the USFS. All of the ranchers thought about this amazing idea for a couple of minutes.

Finally, an old boy in the back stood up, tipped his hat back and said, "Son, I don't think you understand the problem. Those coyotes ain't mating with our sheep - they're eatin' 'em".

Source: Reference No. 7

Getting the Message - 49

In some liturgical churches, each service begins with a greeting. The officiating clergyman says, "The Lord be with you." And the congregation used to respond, "And with thy spirit." But, with the modernizing of the liturgy, the response is now, "The Lord be with you." And everyone says, "And also with you." There is the story of the visiting bishop who went to such a church where the sound system was old and unreliable. He went to the microphone and tapped it several times and finally said, "There's something wrong with this!" and the whole congregation answered, "And also with you."

Source: Reference No. 16

Who is that Idiot? - 50

An itinerant preacher arrived at an outback town in western Queensland and arranged to hold a service in the Mechanics Institute hall the following Sunday afternoon. Then the preacher set about inviting everyone in the area to his meeting. There hadn't been any preaching in that town for as long s anyone could remember, so when the time came to start the service, the small hall was packed. The preacher climbed onto the platform, called for silence and asked if someone could play the piano so they could have some singing before he gave his message. A bloke who occasionally played the piano in the pub volunteered and the some books were handed out.

"Alright," said the preacher, let's begin with an old favorite, song number 4."

"Sorry, Reverend," said the pianist, "I don't know some number 4."

"That's okay," said the enthusiastic preacher, "we'll just sing song number 27. Everybody knows that one." The pianist squirmed a bit on his seat and said, "Sorry, Reverend. I can't play song number 27."

The preacher remaining good-natured, said, "don't fell bad about it, we'll just sing song number 34. Everybody learned that one when they were small children."

The pianist was really nervous by now and said, "Sorry Reverend, but I don't know song 34 either." Where upon, someone at the back shouted, "That pianist is an idiot!"

"Hold it!" exclaimed the preacher, "that wasn't spoken in a spirit of love, I want that man who called the pianist an idiot to stand up." No one stood.

"If he won't stand up, I want one of those sitting next to the man who called the pianist an idiot to stand up." No one moved. After a brief period of complete silence, a little bloke halfway up the hall stood up and said, "Reverend, I didn't call the pianist an idiot. And I'm not sitting next to the man who called the pianist an idiot. What I want to know is, why anyone would think that idiot is a pianist!"

Source: Reference No. 16

Restroom Guidelines - 51

In the past, employees were permitted to make trips to the rest room under informal guidelines. Effective April 1, 1988, a "Rest room Trip Policy" (RTP) will be established to provide a consistent method of accounting for each employee's restroom time and ensuring equal treatment for all employees.

Under this policy, a "Rest room Trip Bank" (RTB) will be established for each employee. The first day of each month, employees will be given a "Rest room Trip Credit" (RTC) of 20. Restroom Trip Credits can be accumulated from month to month.

Currently, the entrances to all rest rooms are being equipped with personal identification stations and computer linked voice print recognition devices. During the next two weeks, each employee must provide the Human Resources Department with two copies of voice prints, (one normal and one under stress) to Personnel. The voice print recognition stations will be operational, but not restrictive, for the next four weeks; employees should acquaint themselves with the stations during that period.

If an employee's RTB balance reaches zero, the doors to the rest rooms will not unlock for that employee's voice until the first of the next month. In addition, all rest room stalls are being equipped with timed paper roll retractors. If the stall is occupied for more than three minutes, an alarm will sound. Thirty seconds after the alarm sounds, the roll of paper in the stall will retract, the toilet will flush, and the stall door will open.

If you have any questions regarding the above policy, please ask your chairperson.

Thank you for your cooperation.

Source: Anonymous

A Vacation - 52

A Chicago salesman called his manager from Miami: "I'm stuck down here. We're in the middle of a hurricane. The planes have stopped flying. The buses and trains aren't running and the highways are flooded. What shall I do?"

"Start your two week vacation as of this morning."

Source: Anonymous

Medical Term - 53

A man told his doctor he wasn't able to do all the things around the house that he used to do. When the examination was over the man said: "Now Doc, I can take it. Tell me in plain English what is wrong with me."

"Well, in plain English, you are just lazy."

"Okay, now give me the medical term so I can tell my wife."

Source: Anonymous

Hillbilly - 54

After living in the remote wilderness of Kentucky all his life, an old hillbilly decided it was time to visit the big city. In one of the stores, he picks up a mirror and looks into it. Not ever having seen one before, he remarked at the image staring back at him, "How about that! Here's a picture of my daddy."

He bought the mirror thinking it was a picture of his daddy, but on the way home, he remembered his wife didn't like his father, so he hung it in the barn, and every morning before leaving for the fields, he would go there and look at it.

His wife began to get suspicious of these many trips to the barn.

One day after her husband left, she searched the barn and found the mirror.

As she looked into the glass, she fumed, "So that's the ugly witch he's runnin' around with."

Source: Reference No. 7

Advice for a Long and Blissful Marriage - 55

At All Saints Lutheran Church in Minneapolis, Minnesota, they have an annual husband's marriage seminar.

At the last session, the Pastor asked Ole Westrum, who was approaching his 50th wedding anniversary, to take a few minutes and share some insight into how he had managed to stay married to the same woman all these years.

"Vell," Ole replied to the assembled husbands, "I've tried to treat her nice, spend da money on her, but best of all, I took her to Norvay for da 20th anniversary!"

The Pastor responded, "Ole, you are an amazing inspiration to all the husbands here! Please tell us what you are planning for your 50th anniversary."

Ole proudly replied, "I'm a-gonna go get her."

Source: Reference No. 7

Cowboy in Church - 56

One Sunday morning, an old cowboy entered a church just before services were to begin. Although the old man and his clothes were spotlessly clean, he wore jeans, a denim shirt and boots that were very worn and ragged. In his hand he carried a worn out old hat and an equally worn out Bible.

The church he entered was in a very upscale and exclusive part of the city. It was the largest and most beautiful church the old cowboy had ever seen. It had high cathedral ceilings, ornate statues, beautiful murals and stained glass windows, plush carpet, and velvet like cushioned pews. The building must have cost many millions of dollars to build and maintain. The men, women and children of the congregation were all dressed in the finest and most expensive suits, dresses, shoes, and jewelry the old cowboy had ever witnessed.

As the poorly dressed cowboy took a seat the others moved away from him. No one greeted him. No one welcomed him. No one offered a handshake. No one spoke to him. They were all appalled at his appearance and did not attempt to hide the fact. There were many glances in his direction as the others frowned and commented amongst themselves about his shabby attire. A few chuckles and giggles came from some of the younger members.

The preacher gave a long sermon about Hellfire and brimstone and a stern lecture on how much money the church needed to do God's work. When the offering plate was passed thousands of dollars came pouring forth.

As soon as the service was over the congregation hurried out. Once again no one spoke or even nodded to the stranger in the ragged clothes and boots. As the old cowboy was leaving the church the preacher approached him. Instead of welcoming him, the preacher asked the cowboy to do him a favor.

"Before you come back in here again, have a talk with God and ask him what He thinks would be appropriate attire for worshiping in this church," the preacher said.

The old cowboy assured the preacher he would do that and left.

The very next Sunday morning the old cowboy showed back up for the services wearing the same ragged jeans, shirt, boots, and hat. Once again the congregation was appalled at his appearance. He was completely shunned and ignored again. The preacher noticed the man still wearing his ragged clothes and boots, and instead of beginning his sermon, stepped down from the pulpit and walked over to where the man sat alone.

"I thought I asked you to speak to God before you came back to our church," the preacher said.

"I did," replied the old cowboy.

"If you spoke to God, what did he tell you the proper attire should be for worshiping in here?" asked the preacher.

"Well, Sir", said the old cowboy, "God told me that He wouldn't have the slightest idea what was appropriate attire for worshiping in your church. He says He's never even been in here before."

Source: Reference No. 7

Disconnect - 57

As a little girl climbed onto Santa's lap, Santa asked the usual, "And what would you like for Christmas?"

The child stared at him open mouthed and horrified for a minute, then gasped, "Didn't you get my email?"

Source: Reference No. 7

New Stock Market Terms - 58

CEO: Chief Embezzlement Officer

CFO: Corporate Fraud Officer

BULL MARKET: A random market movement causing an investor to mistake himself for a financial genius.

BEAR MARKET : A 6 to 18 month period when the kids get no allowance, the wife gets no jewelry.

VALUE INVESTING : The art of buying low and selling lower.

P/E RATIO: The percentage of investors wetting their pants as the market keeps crashing.

BROKER: What my broker has made me.

STANDARD & POOR: Your life in a nutshell.

STOCK ANALYST: Idiot who just downgraded your stock.

STOCK SPLIT: When your ex-wife and her lawyer split your assets equally between themselves.

FINANCIAL PLANNER: A guy whose phone has been disconnected.

MARKET CORRECTION: The day after you buy stocks.

CASH FLOW: The movement your money makes as it disappears down the toilet.

YAHOO: What you yell after selling it to some poor sucker for $240 per share.

WINDOWS: What you jump out of when you're the sucker who bought Yahoo @ $240 per share.

INSTITUTIONAL INVESTOR: Past year investor who's now locked up in a nuthouse.

PROFIT: An archaic word no longer in use.

Source: Reference No. 7

A Tall Order - 59

A woman rubbed an old bottle she found and out popped a genie. The amazed woman asked the genie if it could fulfill three of her wishes. The genie said, "Nope, sorry, three-wish genies are a storybook myth. I'm a one-wish genie. So what'll it be?"

The woman did not hesitate. She said, "I want peace in the Middle East. See this map? I want these countries to stop fighting with each other and I want all the Arabs to love the Jews and Americans and vice-versa. It will bring about world peace and harmony."

The genie looked at the map and exclaimed, "Lady be reasonable. These countries have been at war for thousands of years. I'm out of shape after being in a bottle for five hundred years. I'm good, but not that good! I don't think it can be done. Make another wish and please be reasonable."

The woman thought for a minute and said, "Well, I've never been able to find the right man. You know – one that's considerate and fun, romantic, likes to cook and help with the house cleaning, is good in bed, and gets along well with my family, doesn't watch sports all the time, and is faithful. That is what I wish for... a good man."

The genie let out a long sigh, rolled his eyes and said, "Let me see the fricking map again."

Source: Reference No. 16

ENVIRONMENT

A Paradigm Change for a Family - 60

One Sunday morning on a subway in New York. People were sitting quietly — some reading newspapers, some lost in thought, some resting with their eyes closed. It was a calm, peaceful scene. Then suddenly, a man and his children entered the subway car. The children were so loud and rambunctious that instantly the whole climate changed.

The man sat down next to me and closed his eyes, apparently oblivious to the situation. The children were yelling back and forth, throwing things, even grabbing people's papers. It was very disturbing. And yet, the man sitting next to me did nothing.

It was difficult not to feel irritated. I could not believe that he could be so insensitive to let his children run wild like that and do nothing about it, taking no responsibility at all. It was easy to see that everyone else on the subway felt irritated, too. So finally, with what I felt was unusual patience and restraint, I turned to him and said, "Sir, your children are really disturbing a lot of people. I wonder if you couldn't control them a little more?"

The man lifted his gaze as if to come to a consciousness of the situation for the first time and said softly, "Oh, you're right. I guess I should do something about it. We just came from the hospital where their mother died about an hour ago. I don't know what to think, and I guess they don't know how to handle it either."

Can you imagine what I felt at that moment? My paradigm shifted. Suddenly I saw things differently, I felt differently, I behaved differently. My irritation vanished. I didn't have to worry about controlling my attitude or my behavior; my heart was filled with the man's pain. Feelings of sympathy and compassion flowed freely. "Your wife just died? Oh, I'm so sorry. Can you tell me about it? What can I do to help?" Everything changed in an instant.

Source: Reference No. 1

Common Knowledge - 61

While being driven to another engagement, a professor of nuclear physics who was giving the same special lecture to a number of universities across the country, remarked to his chauffeur, "I suppose you've heard me deliver this lecture so many times now you almost know it by heart." "I think I do, Sir," said the chauffeur and, as if to reassure himself, recited the professor's lecture word-perfectly.

"That's incredible!" exclaimed the professor and then, an idea occurred to him. "Why don't we change places at the next university?" he suggested. "You can wear my suit and gown and I'll put on your uniform and cap. You can give the lecture and I'll sit down at the front and listen for a change ... it'll be our little joke on those fellows and no one else will ever know. What do you think?" "I'll give it a go if you're happy, sir," was the reply.

The necessary changeovers were made and a short time later, when they arrived at the auditorium, the chauffeur, in the professor's gown, was conducted with due ceremony to the platform, introduced and asked to address the assembled academics. The chauffeur obliged by rattling off the lecture and received an enthusiastic ovation from the audience.

Then, to the chauffeur's consternation the chairman proposed that some of those present might wish to put one or two questions to the learned professor. One scientist got to his feet and asked a question that was so theoretical, the chauffeur didn't have the faintest idea what he was asking, let alone what answer to give.

Nevertheless he stepped forward to the rostrum and said, "Frankly, I'm surprised that you should ask me such a simple question. Why, even my chauffeur sitting here in the front row would know the answer to that and to prove it, I'll ask him to step up here now and give you the answer."

Source: Reference No. 16

Dusting - 62

"A house becomes a home when you can write "I love you" on the furniture."

I can't tell you how many countless hours that I have spent CLEANING! I used to spend at least 8 hours every weekend making sure things were just perfect – "in case someone came over." Then I realized one day that no one came over; they were all out living life and having fun!

Now, when people visit, I find no need to explain the "condition" of my home.. They are more interested in hearing about the things I've been doing while I was away living life and having fun. If you haven't figured this out yet, please heed this advice.

Life is short. Enjoy it! Dust if you must, but wouldn't it be better to paint a picture, write a letter, bake a cake or plant a seed, ponder the difference between want and need?

Dust if you must, but there's not much time, with rivers to swim and mountains to climb, music to hear and books to read, friends to cherish and life to lead.

Dust if you must, but the world's out there with the sun in your eyes, the wind in your hair, a flutter of snow, a shower of rain. This day will not come around again.

Dust if you must, but bear in mind, old age will come and it's not kind.

And when you go - and go you must - you, yourself will make more dust!

Share this with all the wonderful women in your life! I Just Did. It's not what you gather, but what you scatter (share) that tells what kind of life you have lived.

Source: Anonymous

Sign of the Times - 63

A dog had followed his owner to school. His owner was a fourth grader at a public elementary school. However, when the bell rang, the dog sidled inside the building and made it all the way to the child's classroom before a teacher noticed and shooed him outside, closing the door behind him.

The dog sat down, whimpered and stared at the closed doors. The God appeared beside the dog, patted his head and said, "Don't feel bad fella'...they won't let me in either."

Source: Reference No. 7

HISTORICAL

An Ohio Woman in the Nineteenth Century - 64

In 1869, a woman in Ohio, USA, was alone in the house on a rainy evening as her husband went to the town store to run errands. The recent family tragedies have added mental sadness to her in addition to this depressing rainy day. The whole day was cloudy and gloomy and it was pouring.

In desperation, this woman kneeled on the floor of her bed room and prayed for the first time in her life. She said "God, I never believed in you and I always questioned your existence although my parents and my siblings always talked about your power. Now I feel totally powerless because none of the medical doctors gave me any reason why both of my boys died just after their births. They just don't know. Now I'm pregnant third time and I'm fearful about the same outcome. I don't have any place to go for the answers and I don't have any doctor who is willing to explain the situation to me. I feel totally lost. God, as a last resort and as a desperate attempt, I'm asking you to come in the process of this third pregnancy and prove your existence to me."

After that prayer, the woman went for a monthly check-up. After the examination, the doctor declared that the head of the baby looks unusually large and baby is likely to be abnormal. After that diagnosis, the devastated woman started praying (desperately and regularly) and begging for God's help, just in case there was a God.

This process, her monthly examinations and the declaration by the doctor that the baby's head was large and her praying regularly, continued until the baby was delivered.

Fortunately, the delivery turned out to be uncomplicated, but, as the doctor predicted, the baby's head was larger than normal and the woman had a boy with a large head.

In the school the boy was known as a large head boy, but to America and to the world, this boy became known as the most creative American inventor who has earned maximum number of patents so far. He is well-known for his inventions such as the, light bulb, cement concrete, etc., etc.

This American with an unusually large head is known as Thomas Edison who was born in 1869 in Ohio to a woman who begged for a divine intervention a year before when her two previous boys died after birth without any reason or any explanation.

Historians continue to make a point that big head of Thomas Edison was responsible for his creativity and for securing the maximum number of patents than any American so far. Some people had believed and claimed that the big head is a result of divine intervention when the woman specifically asked for the divine assistance.

Source: Reference No. 5

The Chairman and the Secrets - 65

A college student in St. Louis, Missouri, USA, was a very plain speaking and intelligent person. His social skills were extraordinary. Noticing this young man with great social skills, his College Professor suggested him to consider public service as his career. The young man agreed and ran for a Senate seat and he was elected to the US Senate.

This Senator was so good that he was immediately selected as the Chairman of the Senate National Security Council, which was the most powerful Senate committee at the time in the United States.

As a first duty of the new Chairman, the Senator was given a list of 80 projects that needed to be approved by the Chairman. Among the 80 projects and their costs, the Chairman noticed an item with the cost equal to the sum of other items. When the Chairman asked for more information about the project, he was asked to keep his mouth shut. Being a powerful Chairman, he asked again about it and he was requested to approve the project without asking anymore questions. For four consecutive years, the Senator and his committee approved the most expensive project without knowing anything about the project. Next following year, the Senator became the Vice President, then President the next year when the incumbent President died in the office.

After becoming the President, he had to implement the results of that project. On the 102nd day after being sworn in as President, he decided to implement the results of the project and he dropped the first Atomic Bomb over Nagasaki and Hiroshima (Japan) in 1945.

That Senator and President was Harry Truman and the project was known as the Manhattan Project (of building and atomic bomb).

Source: Reference No. 5

Paradigm Changes About the Father in the Lifetime - 66

The first characteristic of a paradigm is that it is a dynamic concept. That means it is constantly changing. It is common for people to change their perception or thinking or even the model. This point is illustrated by the following observations by an unnamed person.

When I was 4 years old, I thought that my father could do anything.

When I was 7 years old, I thought, my dad knows a lot, a whole lot.

When I was 12 years old, I thought, my dad doesn't know quite everything.

When I was 21 years old, I thought, Oh, that man is out of date, what did you expect?

When I was 30 years old, I thought, my dad knows a little bit about it, but not much.

When I was 40 years old, I thought, let's get dad's assessment before we do anything.

When I was 60 years old, I thought, my dad knew absolutely everything!

When I was 65 years old, I thought, I'd give anything if dad were here so I could talk this over with him. I really missed him.

Source: Reference No. 14

Math Progression - 67

Teaching Math in 1950's: A logger sells a truckload of lumber for $100. His cost of production is 4/5 of the price. What is his profit?

Teaching Math in 1960's: A logger sells a truckload of lumber for $100. His cost of production is 4/5 of the price, or $80. What is his profit?

Teaching Math in 1970's: A logger exchanges a set "L" of lumber for a set "M" of money. The cardinality of set "M" is 100. Each element is worth one dollar. Make 100 dots representing the elements of the set "M". The set "C", the cost of production contains 20 fewer points than set "M". Represent the set "C" as a subset of set "M" and answer the following question: What is the cardinality of the set "P" of profits?

Teaching Math in 1980's: A logger sells a truckload of lumber for $100. His cost of production is $80 and his profit is $20. Your assignment: Underline the number 20.

Teaching Math in 1990's: By cutting down beautiful forest trees, the logger makes $20. What do you think of this way of making a living? Topic for class participation after answering the question: How did the forest birds and squirrels feel as the logger cut down the trees? There are no wrong answers.

Source: Reference No. 7

An Oversight by the President of Harvard University - 68

A lady in a faded gingham dress and her husband, dressed

in a homespun threadbare suit, stepped off the train in Boston, and walked timidly without an appointment into the president's outer office. The secretary could tell in a moment that such backwoods, country hicks had no business at Harvard and probably didn't even deserve to be in Cambridge. She frowned.

"We want to see the president," the man said softly.

"He'll be busy all day," the secretary snapped.

"We'll wait," the lady replied.

For hours the secretary ignored them, hoping that the couple would finally become discouraged and go away. They didn't. And the secretary grew frustrated and finally decided to disturb the president, even though it was a chore she always regretted to do.

"Maybe if they just see you for a few minutes, they'll leave," she told him. And he sighed in exasperation and nodded. Someone of his importance obviously didn't have the time to spend with them, but he detested gingham dresses and homespun suits cluttering up his outer office. The president stern-faced with dignity, strutted toward the couple.

The lady told him, "We had a son that attended Harvard for one year. He loved Harvard. He was happy here. But about a year ago, he was accidentally killed. And my husband and I would like to erect a memorial to him, somewhere on campus."

The president wasn't touched, he was shocked. "Madam," he said gruffly, "We can't put up a statue for every person who attended Harvard and died. If we did, this place would look like a cemetery."

"Oh no," the lady explained quickly, "We don't want to erect a statue. We thought we would like to give a building to Harvard."

The president rolled his eyes. He glanced at the gingham dress and homespun suit, then exclaimed, "A building! Do you have any earthly idea how much a building costs? We have over seven and a half million dollars in the physical plant at Harvard."

For a moment the lady was silent. The president was pleased. He could get rid of them now. And the lady turned to her husband and said quietly, "Is that all it costs to start a University? Why don't we just start our own? Her husband nodded. The president's face wilted in confusion and bewilderment. And Mr. and Mrs. Leland Stanford walked away, traveling to Palo Alto, California where they established the University that bears their name, a memorial to a son that Harvard no longer cared about.

Source: Reference No. 6

A Dream - 69

One night I had a dream.

I dreamed I was walking along with the Lord and across the sky flashed scenes of my life. For each scene I noticed two sets of footprints in the sand, one belonging to me, the other to the Lord.

When the last scene of my life flashed before us, I looked back at the footprints in the sand I noticed that many times along the path of my life there was only one set of footprints

I also noticed that it happened at the very lowest and saddest times of my life. This really bothered me and I questioned the Lord about it "Lord, you said that once I decided to follow you, you would walk with me all the way, but I have noticed that during the most troublesome times of my life, there is only one set of footprints. I don't understand why, in times when I needed you most, you would leave me."

The Lord replied, "My precious child, I love you and I would never, never leave you. During your times of trials and suffering, when you see only one set of footprints, it was then that I carried you."

Source: Anonymous

HUMAN BEHAVIOR

The Man and the Lottery - 70

A religious man was praying God every day that he will be a lottery winner. He prayed everyday as much as four times a day. Nothing happened for days, weeks and months and years.

Finally, God responded to his prayers and said, "Son, you have to do your part first. You have to buy the lottery ticket first."

Source: Anonymous

A Story of Ray Doss - 71

I am going to share a confession with you. It is something that I have never been proud of. When I graduated college and from seminary, I became the pastor of a little church in Ivanhoe, Illinois. To build up the church, I rang doorbells. And every time someone answered, if they were not already committed to another church, I would write down their name and address and put them on the mailing list of the church.

One day, I rang the doorbell of a house. It was to be an experience which, fifty years later, I still vividly remember. A man opened the door. It was three in the afternoon, and he had a can of beer in his hand. It was obvious that he had already had too much to drink. I told him who I was, and he asked me to come in. He asked me to sit down. Then he said to me, "I never had a preacher in my house before, but then again, I've never been to church either." I was shocked!

"Never?" I asked. Then he thought a moment and recalled, "Well, I think when I was a kid I went to Sunday school once or twice." So I asked him, "Why don't you go to church?" That was the wrong question! He launched into a tirade against preachers. The priests were bad…the preachers were bad…

and the rabbis were a bunch of hypocrites (so he informed me). Then he added, "I do business with the people who go to your church. They tell lies. They're dishonest. They steal from me." He went on and on and on. I had no chance to defend anything or anyone. Every time I tried to ask him a question, he interrupted with rude and nasty responses.

Being young and immature, finally I did something I probably should not have done.

I jumped to my feet and asked, "Don't you believe in Heaven or Hell?" He said, "No." Then I said it! I said, "Well, go to hell then!" And I ran out and slammed the door. I should not have said it! It was awful. Can you imagine me doing that? Well, I had written his name and address down on my mailing list.

Now I scratched through it and went home trembling and terribly upset. My wife quickly questioned my behavior. "What's wrong?" she quizzed. I explained it all. She looked at me aghast. "You said what to him?" Her mouth hung open. I repeated my confession. She sighed. "Oh, Bob! How could you do that?" I said, "I don't know, but I did."

God did not send his son into the world to condemn the world, but that the world, through Him, might be saved! That's not what I communicated. I condemned the poor man. I confess. I am not proud of it. Fortunately, two weeks after our meeting, he came to church. He was wearing a suit and tie. He was sober. I shook hands with him at the door and said, "Good to see you, Ray." (Thank God, I remembered his name.) The next Sunday, he returned… and the next… and the next. Three months later, he came to the front of the church, knelt there, and said to me, "Reverend, will you baptize me?" He was crying. I said, "Sure." And without a planned ceremony, I baptized him.

After that, this man began coming to Bible study and studied the Ten Commandments and the teachings of Jesus Christ. He turned into a beautiful, transformed person. He actually became a licensed preacher. Preaching became his new profession, until years later when he retired. I had long since left

Chicago and was in California building this church when my secretary buzzed my office and said, "There's someone here to see you, Dr. Schuller. He says his name is Ray Doss. Do you know him?" I couldn't believe it. It was the same man, now a dear friend. We had a wonderful reunion. He said to me, "I want to move here and, for the rest of my life, full time, I want to work as a volunteer for the pastor who led me to Jesus Christ."

So he was a volunteer for this church for a long time. If you walked across the lawn, Ray Doss had mowed it. If you used the bathroom, he had cleaned it. He worked until he became too ill with cancer. As he was dying, I went to say goodbye, and he smiled and said, "Rev. (which he always called me), I'm goin'..." I interrupted him, "I know Ray." And then he smiled, and he said, "I know where I'm goin' and it's not going to be where you told me to go." We laughed and cried and embraced.

Source: Reference No. 9

Who Thinks He Can - 72

If you think you are beaten, you are,
If you think you dare not, you don't
If you like to win, but think you can't,
It is almost certain you won't.

If you think you'll lose, you're lost,
For out in the world we find,
Success begins with a fellow's will –
It is all in the state of mind.

If you think you are outclassed, you are,
You've got to think high to rise,
You've got to be sure of yourself before
You can ever win a prize.

Life's battles don't always go
To the stronger or faster man.
For sooner or later the person who wins
Is the person Who Thinks He Or She Can!

Source: Anonymous

Divorce vs. Murder - 73

A nice calm and respectable lady went into the pharmacy, walked up to the pharmacist, looked straight into his eyes, and said, "I would like to buy some cyanide."

The pharmacist asked, "Why in the world do you need cyanide?"

The lady replied, "I need it to poison my husband."

The pharmacist's eyes got big and he exclaimed, "Lord have mercy! I can't give you cyanide to kill your husband! That's against the law! I'll lose my license! They'll throw both of us in jail! All kinds of bad things will happen. Absolutely not! You CANNOT have any cyanide!"

The lady reached into her purse and pulled out a picture of her husband, in bed with the pharmacist's wife.

The pharmacist looked at the picture and replied, "Well now, that's different. You didn't tell me you had a pre-scription."

Source: Reference No. 7

Points to Ponder - 74

Don't worry about what people think; they don't do it very often.

Going to church doesn't make you a Christian anymore than standing in a garage makes you a car.

Artificial intelligence is no match for natural stupidity.

Not one shred of evidence supports the notion that life is serious.

A person, who is nice to you, but rude to the waiter, is not a nice person. (This is very important. Pay attention! It never fails.)

For every action, there is an equal and opposite government program.

Bills travel through the mail at twice the speed of checks.

A conscience is what hurts when all of your other parts feel so good.

No man had ever been shot while doing the dishes.

Opportunities always look bigger after they have passed.

Junk is something you've kept for years and throw away three weeks before you need it.

There is always one more imbecile that you counted on.

Experience is a wonderful thing. It enables you to recognize a mistake when you make it again.

By the time you can make ends meet, they move the ends.

Someone who thinks logically provides a nice contrast to the real world.

It ain't the jeans that make your butt look fat.

There is a very fine line between 'hobby' and 'mental illness'.

You should not confuse your career with your life

The most destructive force in the universe is gossip.

Never be afraid to try something new. Remember that a lone amateur built the Ark. A large group of professionals built the Titanic.

Source: Reference No. 7

INSPIRATIONAL

The Classical Letter of a Boy of Six, Written 35 Years Later... - 75

John Hobb was a very distinguished British clergyman. He was a most admired religious leader in Britain during the nineteenth century. He was a household name, just like Billy Graham is in USA.

When he was a small boy, only six years old, his father and mother died and he was left an only child, orphaned.

At the funeral, he was handed a letter from his aunt, whom he had never met and who lived a long distance away. She wrote, "John, come live with me. I'm your aunt. I love you. I'll be your mother and father."

So instead of going to an orphanage, he went to live with his aunt. She gave him advantages he never had. She was rich.

He attended the University. He obtained a theological education and became a distinguished clergyman.

One day, years after this, at the age of 41 years old, he received a letter from his aunt, whom he had not seen for decades. The letter said, "John, this is the second time I have written you a letter, so you know it's important." She wrote on, "The doctor tells me I have cancer and shall soon die. John, I'm no scholar like you are. What lies ahead for me?"

John wrote his aunt a letter which has become a classic piece of literature. The letter is called "The Letter of a Little Boy of Six, Written 35 Years Later".

It reads:

Dear Auntie. It is now 35 years since I, a little boy of six, was left alone in the world. You sent me word that you would give me a home and be a kind mother to me.

I've never forgotten the day when I made that long journey to your home. I can still recall my disappointment when I learned that instead of coming for me yourself, you sent a hired man to fetch me.

I can still remember my tears, as perched on a horse, I clung tightly to the back of John, your hired man, as we started off to my new home. Night fell before we finished the journey.

As the darkness deepened, I began to be afraid. I said to the man in front of me, "Do you think she'll go to bed before I get there?"

And he said, throwing his head back to me as the horse trotted on, "Oh, no. She'll surely stay up for you, Johnny. When we get out of these woods, you'll see her candle lit."

As we rode into a clearing, there, sure enough, I did see a friendly candle in the window. I remember that you were waiting in the door. You put your arms around me and lifted me, a tired, frightened boy. You lifted me down from the horse.

I remember there was a bright fire in the hearth (in the kitchen) and a warm supper on the stove and after supper, you took me up to the room and heard me say my prayers. Then you sat beside me until I fell asleep.

You're probably wondering why I'm recalling all of this now.

Auntie, well, your letter reminded me of it. For one day soon, God will send for you to take you to your new home. Don't fear the summons or the strange journey or the messenger.

At the end of the road, you'll see a light in the window, and standing in the open doorway, smiling at you, will be your God. You will be safe forevermore. Auntie, God can be trusted to be as kind to you as you were to me 35 years ago.

This is a letter of a little boy of six, written 35 years later…

Source: Reference No. 10

What Is Life? - 76

Life is a challenge…meet it.
Life is a gift…accept it.
Life is an adventure…dare it.

Life is a sorrow…overcome it.
Life is a tragedy…face it.
Life is a duty…perform it.
Life is a game…play it.
Life is a mystery…unfold it.
Life is a song…sing it.
Life is an opportunity…take it.
Life is a journey…complete it.
Life is a promise…fulfill it.
Life is a beauty…praise it.
Life is a struggle…fight it.
Life is a goal…achieve it.
Life is a puzzle…solve it.
Life is a Love…love it!
Life is a ride…enjoy it.

Source: Anonymous

George Patton's one Minute Message - 77

Speak up – make yourself be heard. If you expect your soldiers to act bravely, you'd better act bravely yourself. If you expect your men to dress, act and think like soldiers, you'd better dress, act and think like one yourself.

You can't be just a good soldier, you must be a better soldier than every one of your subordinates. If you're not the best soldier in your unit, you shouldn't be in charge. You must be able to do everything your soldiers do, and you must do it better than any of them.

Excuses are not acceptable.

Source: Anonymous

$20.00 - 78

A well-known speaker started off his seminar by holding up a $20.00 bill. In the room of 200, he asked, "Who would like this $20 bill?"

Hands started going up. He said, "I am going to give this $20 to one of you, but first, let me do this." He proceeded to crumple up the $20 dollar bill. He then asked, "Who still wants it?" Still the hands were up in the air.

"Well," he replied, "What if I do this?" And he dropped it on the ground and started to grind it into the floor with his shoe. He picked it up, now crumpled and dirty.

"Now, who still wants it?" Still the hands went into the air.

"My friends, we have all learned a very valuable lesson. No matter what I did to the money, you still wanted it because it did not decrease in value. It was still worth $20," he said. "Many times in our lives, we are dropped, crumpled, and ground into the dirt by the decisions we make and the circumstances that come our way. We feel as though we are worthless. But no matter what has happened or what will happen, you will never lose your value. Dirty or clean, crumpled or finely creased, you are still priceless to those who DO LOVE you. The worth of our lives comes not in what we do or who we know, but by WHO WE ARE and WHOSE WE ARE. You are special - Don't EVER forget it."

Source: Reference No. 7

A Word by Rudyard Kipling - 79

Rudyard Kipling was one of those authors who was very successful in his lifetime. A British newspaper criticized him and ridiculed him and called him a mercenary. They said, "He is now writing just for the money. One word of Rudyard Kipling today is worth a hundred dollars."

Shortly after the release of the unkind article, a reporter approached Kipling at a gathering and said, "So, you're worth a hundred dollars a word. Here's a hundred dollars. Give me a word." Then he handed him a paper and pencil.

Kipling took the hundred dollars, put it in his pocket, and on the paper, he wrote one word: Thanks!

Source: Reference No. 12

MISCELLANEOUS

A Well Kept Secret in Washington D.C. – 80

A young British woman visited France in 1765 and flirted with some of the French Military Officers. As a result, James Macey was born in France in 1765. He was declared a illegitimate child in his birth-certificate.

Several days after James Macey was born, his mother with little James, moved to England. Right from the day James Macey arrived in England, his illegitimate status followed. He was denied admission to good schools, he could not make any friends, no social life, not allowed on playgrounds, no jobs as a kids and on and on.

James Macey was good and creative in Arts and Science subjects. He worked very hard to develop numerous experiments. The papers based on his work were never accepted for publication in 1800. He could not meet the prospective girls and thus remained unmarried throughout his adult life. His own hard work and love for Arts and Sciences allowed him to accumulate a very large sum of money in spite of the fact that he was discriminated against at every level because of the stigma of illegitimacy at the time. He died in 1828.

During his last years, he became somewhat bitter toward England by realizing the great injustice that was forced upon him for the action over which he had no control. He decided to give all his fortune to a country other than England which mistreated his so much. Also, stigma was constantly attached to his name so he had to change his name before donating that huge amount of money.

James Macey selected the USA as the country to donate the money to. His donated money was used to build a large institute in the USA. The new name he took was Smithsonian. The Smithsonian Institute of Arts and Sciences in Washington, D.C., is now the world's best museum that was built entirely by James Macey donations (under the disguised name of

Smithsonian). This institute has been visited and enjoyed by millions and millions of people for over 170 years.

Source: Reference No. 5

A Cross-Examination - 81

A defense attorney was cross-examining a police officer during a felony trial - it went like this:

Q. Officer, did you see my client fleeing the scene?

A. No sir, but I subsequently observed a person matching the description of the offender running several blocks away.

Q. Officer, who provided this description?

A. The officer who responded to the scene.

Q. A fellow officer provided the description of this so-called offender. Do you trust your fellow officers?

A. Yes sir, with my life.

Q. With your life? Let me ask you this then officer - do you have a locker room in the police station - a room where you change your clothes in preparation for you daily duties?

A. Yes sir, we do.

Q. And do you have a locker in that room?

A. Yes sir, I do.

Q. And do you have a lock on your locker?

A. Yes sir.

Q. Now why is it, officer, if you trust your fellow officers with your life, that you find it necessary to lock your locker in a room you share with those same officers?

A. You see sir, we share the building with a court complex, and sometimes lawyers have been known to walk through that room.

Source: Reference No. 7

Thirteen Things that the American High School Graduates Have Not Learnt in the School - 82

Life is not fair. Get used to it.

Life would care about you only after significant accomplishments. Try to accomplish big things. Attempt to do big things and fail than do nothing and succeed.

You will not get 40,000 dollars job right away.

Get ready for those bosses (and Professors) who have tenures and play games on other people's life and careers.

Flipping hamburgers is an opportunity to work while finishing the education.

Don't blame parents. They were here before you were born.

Your parents become boring because they are tired of paying your bills.

Schools can make changes that make you feel good about your education artificially. This is not practiced in the workplace where cut-throat competition is common in modern times.

Television is not real life.

Get ready for nerds who are found more frequently in workplaces than in the school environment.

Smoking will not make you cool, instead, it will make you look like a moron.

Living fast and carelessly makes people live shorter.

Get up when you fall down. Michael Jordan confessed that 13,000 times he did not succeed throwing the ball in the basket. He lost 243 games. His team lost 22 times because of his personal failure to score the points during the last seconds of the ballgames.

Source: Reference No. 5

Leave Statistics - 83

Before You Ask Me For A Day Off, consider The Following Statistics:

There are 365 days in a year.

You sleep eight hours in a day making 122 days, which subtracted from 365 days makes 243 days.

You also have 8 hours recreation every day making another 122 days leaving a balance of 121 days.

There are 52 Sundays that you do not work at all which leaves 69 days.

You get Saturday afternoon off.

This gives 52 half-days, or 26 more days that you do not work, this leaves a balance of 43 days.

You get an hour off for lunch, which when totaled makes 16 days, leaving 27 days of the year. You get at least 21 days leave every year, so that leaves 6 days.

You get 5 legal holidays during the year, which leaves only one day

And I'll Be Damned If I'll Give You That One Day Off!!!

Source: Anonymous

30 Years Difference! - 84

1972: Long hair
2002: Longing for hair
1972: KEG
2002: EKG
1972: Acid rock
2002: Acid reflux
1972: Moving to California because it's cool
2002: Moving to California because it's warm
1972: Trying to look like Marlon Brando or Liz Taylor
2002: Trying NOT to look like Marlon Brando or Liz Taylor
1972: Hoping for a BMW
2002: Hoping for a BM
1972: The Grateful Dead
2002: Dr. Kevorkian
1972: Going to a new, hip joint
2002: Receiving a new hip joint
1972: Rolling Stones
2002: Kidney Stones
1972: Being called into the principal's office
2002: Calling the principal's office

1972: Disco
2002: Costco
1972: Parents begging you to get your hair cut
2002: Children begging you to get their heads shaved
1972: Passing the drivers' test
2002: Passing the vision test
1972: Whatever
2002: Depends

Source: Anonymous

What's the Problem? - 85

The professor walked into the classroom and wrote three numbers on the blackboard: 3, 6, 12. Then he turned to the class and asked: "What is the solution?"

"It's a progression," said a boy. "The next number is 24."

"No." said the professor.

"Add them up and you'll get 21," said a girl.

The professor shook his head.

"2167" somebody shouted from the back.

"No, no, no," said the professor. "The correct answer is: "What's the problem?" I did not state the problem but you rushed to find solutions. How can you find a solution unless you know the exact problem?"

The class nodded in agreement.

"Now let's try again," said the professor.

He turned to the board and wrote 23 41 82.

When he turned around the class roared: "What's the problem?"

"I don't see any problem," said the professor smiling. "This is my telephone number. My second advice to you is: Stay relaxed. Don't get tense over imaginary problems.

Source: Anonymous

Trick Dog - 86

A man walks into a bar with his dog. He sits down at the bar and orders a beer. The bartender tells the man that it is a nice looking dog and asks if he knows any tricks.

The man says, "Yes," and tells the dog, "The Gators beat the Noles today." The dog stands up on its hind legs and starts swaying back and forth while barking. "We are the boys from Old Florida."

The bartender says, "Hey, that is pretty good. What happens if you tell him the Noles beat Florida?"

The man replies, "I don't know, he's only 5 years old."

Source: Reference No. 7

Things you'd Love to Say at Work, but Can't! - 87

I don't know what your problem is, but I'll bet it's hard to pronounce.

How about never? Is never good for you?

I'll try being nicer if you'll try being smarter.

I like you. You remind me of when I was young and stupid.

You are validating my inherent mistrust of strangers.

I have plenty of talent and vision. I just don't give a damn.

I'm already visualizing the duct tape over your mouth.

I will always cherish the initial misconceptions I had about you.

Thank you. We're all refreshed and challenged by your unique point of view.

Any connection between your reality and mine is purely coincidental.

What am I? Flypaper for freaks!?

Do I look like a people person?

This isn't an office. It's Hell with fluorescent lighting.

I started out with nothing and still have most of it left.

How do I set a laser printer to stun?

Source: Reference No. 7

Grocery List - 88

Louise Redden, a poorly dressed lady with a look of defeat on her face, walked into a grocery store. She approached the owner of the store in a most humble manner and asked if he would let her charge a few groceries.

She softly explained that her husband was very ill and unable to work, they had seven children and they needed food.

John Longhouse, the grocer, scoffed at her and requested that she leave his store at once.

Visualizing the family needs, she said: "Please, sir! I will bring you the money just as soon as I can."

John told her he could not give her credit, since she did not have a charge account at his store. Standing beside the counter was a customer who overheard the conversation between the two. The customer walked forward and told the grocer that he would stand good for whatever she needed for her family.

The grocer said in a very reluctant voice, "Do you have a grocery list?"

Louise replied, "Yes sir." "O. K." he said, "put your grocery list on the scales and whatever your grocery list weighs, I will give you that amount in groceries."

Louise, hesitated a moment with a bowed head, then she reached into her purse and took out a piece of paper and scribbled something on it. She then laid the piece of paper on the scale carefully with her head still bowed. The grocer and the customer's eyes showed amazement when the scales went down and stayed down.

The grocer, staring at the scales, turned slowly to the customer and said begrudgingly, "I can't believe it."

The customer smiled and the grocer started putting the groceries on the other side of the scales. The scale did not balance so he continued to put more and more groceries on them until the scales would hold no more.

The grocer stood there in utter disgust. Finally, he grabbed the piece of paper from the scales and looked at it with greater amazement. It was not a grocery list, it was a prayer, which said:

"Dear Lord, you know my needs and I am leaving this in your hands."

The grocer gave her the groceries that he had gathered and stood in stunned silence. Louise thanked him and left the store. The other customer handed a fifty-dollar bill to the grocer and said; "It was worth every penny of it. Only God Knows how much a prayer weighs."

Source: Reference No. 7

The Duck & the Lawyer - 89

A big city lawyer went duck hunting in rural Tennessee. He shot and dropped a bird, but it fell into a farmer's field on the other side of a fence. As the lawyer climbed over the fence, an elderly farmer drove up on his tractor and asked him what he was doing.

The attorney responded, "I shot a duck and it fell in this field, and now I'm going to retrieve it."

The old farmer replied, "This is my property, and you are not coming over here."

The indignant lawyer said, "I am one of the best trial attorneys in the United States and, if you don't let me get that duck, I'll sue you and take everything you own."

The old farmer smiled and said, "Apparently, you don't know how we settle disputes in Tennessee. We settle small disagreements with the 'Three Kick Rule'.

The lawyer asked, "What is the Three Kick Rule"?

The Farmer replied, "Well, because the dispute occurs on my land, I get to go first. I kick you three times and then you kick me three times, and so on back and forth until someone gives up."

The attorney quickly thought about the proposed contest and decided that he could easily take the old codger. He agreed to abide by the local custom.

The old farmer slowly climbed down from the tractor and walked up to the attorney. His first kick planted the toe of his heavy steel-toed work boot into the lawyer's groin and dropped him to his knees. His second kick to the midriff sent the lawyer's last meal gushing from his mouth. The lawyer was on all fours when the farmer's third kick to his rear end, sent him face-first into a fresh cow pie.

The lawyer summoned every bit of his will and managed to get to his feet. Wiping his face with the arm of his jacket, he said, "Okay, you old fart. Now it's my turn."

The old farmer smiled and said, "Nah, I give up. You can have the duck."

Source: Reference No. 7

MOTIVATIONAL

Fleming and Churchill Interactions - 90

His name was Fleming, and he was a poor Scottish farmer. One day, while trying to make a living for his family, he heard a cry for help coming from a nearby bog. He dropped his tools and ran to the bog. There, mired to his waist in black muck, was a terrified boy, screaming and struggling to free himself.

Farmer Fleming saved the lad from what could have been a slow and terrifying death.

The next day, a fancy carriage pulled up to the Scotsman's sparse surroundings. An elegantly dressed nobleman stepped out and introduced himself as the father of the boy Farmer Fleming had saved.

"I want to repay you," said the nobleman. "You saved my son's life." "No, I can't accept payment for what I did," the Scottish farmer replied, waving off the offer.

At that moment, the farmer's own son came to the door of the family hovel.

"Is that your son?" the nobleman asked.

"Yes," the farmer replied proudly.

"I'll make you a deal. Let me provide him with the level of education my son will enjoy. If the lad is anything like his father, he'll no doubt grow to be a man we both will be proud of." And that he did.

Farmer Fleming's son attended the very best schools and in time, he graduated from St. Mary's Hospital Medical School in London, and went on to become known throughout the world as the noted Sir Alexander Fleming, the discoverer of Penicillin.

Years afterward, the same nobleman's son who was saved from the bog was stricken with pneumonia. What saved his life this time?

Penicillin.
The name of the nobleman? Lord Randolph Churchill.
His son's name? Sir Winston Churchill.

Source: Reference No. 8

The Pies in Venice, Florida - 91

Late Dr. Norman Vince Peale was invited to speak in Tampa. After his speaking engagement, he and his brother were on the way to Tampa Airport. Since they had some time, at the suggestion of his brother, they stopped in Venice to taste the best pie in the world.

Venice is a small town but the pie shop was full. They tasted the pie and Dr. Peale admitted that it was the best pie he had tasted because Dr. Peale had traveled all over the world during the last five decades.

After finishing the pie and before the leaving the place, he wanted to know who was baking the delicious pies.

"Who is behind this?"

When he asked that question he was taken in the kitchen, which was very clean and he was introduced to a lady who was owner of the place and who was the brain behind the pie.

During the Conversation, Dr. Peale came to know that this elderly lady started her business after her husband died when she was 65 years old. She was a house wife all these years. She did not have any education or skills that she could capitalize on. So she prayed to God and asked for divine guidance regarding her future living.

At that time, she remembered that everybody liked her pies. She was very good in baking pies. That thought or idea came from God and then she started the business and it was growing right in the middle of Venice which is not known to many, even to many Floridians.

In this world, when you see an extraordinary thing, there is likelihood that divine guidance played an important role in its development.

Without divine guidance, the people in Tampa would not have had a taste of the best pie in the world.

Source: Reference No. 13

Need Help - 92

Lord, I have been so good today. I haven't raised my voice to anyone. I haven't called anyone rude names. I haven't yelled and screamed, ranted and raved at anyone. I haven't even broken anything or hurt anybody. But Lord, I'm getting out of bed in about five minutes and I will probably need your help then.

Source: Anonymous

I Am a Fortunate Man - 93

Few others enjoy the freedom that I sometimes take for granted. On this farm, I answer to only one man-the same man I look at in the mirror at the beginning of every day! I spend my days doing what I love and my nights surrounded by family and friends. I am truly blessed.

I do not own this land anymore than it owns me. I am only its steward. I will use the land wisely; and do my part to improve it. Caring for it until the time has come to pass it on to the next generation. And I will do my part to teach them the same respect I have learned.

I have learned the nature of business and strive to understand the business of nature. Peaks and valleys compose the natural cycle of farming. I won't get carried away by a peak, or destroyed by a valley. I will move steadily on. Tomorrow I will return to finish what I didn't accomplish today. I will rest when the work is done.

I have never asked for recognition. Not even a thank you. I am proud of what I do, and that is all I need. I don't farm with the hope that I will get noticed. I farm because it is what I was called to do, and I can't imagine doing anything else.

I must plan and prepare for the future even though I can only speculate at what it will bring. I will keep an eye on the future and a foot in the past. To continue to feed a growing world, I must seek out and embrace new, more efficient technologies and business practices that give me an edge. I will not only survive: I will succeed. I will hold my head high, because I am a farmer.

A very fortunate man.

Source: Reference No. 7

MYSTERIOUS

A Story of the Famous American Singer - 94

Ninety-six years ago (the year was 1916), a young couple in Hoboken, New Jersey, was expecting their first baby. Husband and wife were very happy. The mother of the wife was particularly happy because her ninth and youngest child was going to have her first baby. The couple was very confident that their first child was going to be a girl because both of them like baby girls. After looking through a long list of girl names, they finally selected "Natalie" as the name for their baby girl.

When that final day came, mother noticed that the baby was not moving. She was immediately taken to the hospital and the doctors examined the mother declaring that the baby was dead and they proceeded to perform a C-section to remove the baby and to save the mother's life.

After the operation, a dead baby, a hurting mother and the grandmother were the only people in the hospital room. The grandmother stared at the dead baby, grimly. All of a sudden, she remembered something that she had heard a long time ago. She immediately took that dead baby, shook it a bit and put it under the running cold water from a near-by faucet. Ten seconds passed and nothing happened. The mother pulled the baby out and shook it again and put it back under colder water. After twenty seconds, the baby burped. The air that choked the baby was removed and the baby started breathing again.

That baby was a boy instead of a girl. The couple did not have a name picked for a boy, so in a hurry, they gave the name, "Francis" to the baby. The baby boy did not like the name Francis. So, he selected his own name, "Frank Sinatra".

Source: Reference No. 5

Amy - 95

On Saturday, early morning, Amy knew that her symptoms were coming back. Amy was suffering from a severe Asthma which was a result of allergies affecting her lung tissue.

She told her mother about it. Her mother started preparing to take Amy to the emergency room of the local hospital where she is well known for her severe illness.

While getting ready, her mother started blaming herself for the problem. Her mother said that if she had cleaned her room three times a day instead of two times a week, this would not have happened, and on and on.

Again, Amy was taken to the hospital as usual. But this time there was a new medical doctor who examined her and reviewed her medical file.

The doctor said to her mother that he had an idea that he wanted to try out. He suggested that Amy should start swimming. Her mother replied, "Doctor, are you crazy? Do you know that for the whole of last year, Amy was not able to sit or stand upright in one place because her lungs were collapsing? Swimming is just impossible," she said.

The doctor requested that she let Amy begin very slowly. The first week, Amy could not swim more than 1 foot. The second week, Amy learnt to swim 10 feet. The more she swam, the more she liked it and the more she became healthier. Within ten to fifteen years, she became so proficient that she set a new record in swimming by winning the maximum number of gold medals in the Olympics for the United States.

This success was a result of many factors. But the significant factor was the doctor's judgment that the chlorine added to the swimming pool was of a higher quantity in comparison to the chlorine in drinking water. Chlorine, a known and powerful oxidant, was able to eliminate the infection by disinfecting Amy's lungs and body. Amy got better due to the exercise but the disinfectant property of the chlorine used in the swimming pool really made her healthier because the chlorine killed all the bugs that were the main causes of her allergies.

The female, record setting Olympic gold medallist swimmer is known to the world as Amy VanDyken.

Strange Decision Criteria - 96

A tourist walked down a pier and watched a fisherman pull in a large fish, measure it, and throw it back. He caught a second fish, smaller this time, measured it, and put it in his bucket. Oddly, all the large fish that he caught that measured more, he discarded. All fish smaller than ten inches, he kept. Puzzled, the curious onlooker questioned,

"Pardon me, but why do you keep the little ones and throw the big ones away?" The old fellow looked up and without blinking an eye, he said,

"Why, because my frying pan measures only ten inches across!"

Source: Reference No. 12

Another Strange Decision Criteria - 97

The ground water monitoring for pesticides has just begun in mid-80s. The state of Florida was developing the scientific framework for selecting the county for ground water monitoring for pesticides in Florida. The framework for such selection has numerous scientific factors and it turned out to be a sophisticated and complicated scientific procedure. The procedure was applied in Florida successfully in selecting counties for ground water monitoring so that the probability of detecting pesticides in ground water wells is high. At the same time, a federal agency launched its nationwide survey program for selecting counties for ground water for pesticides.

Among over four thousand counties of the USA, the federal agency selected the Lake County in Florida as the first county for monitoring ground water for pesticides. Obviously, the Florida scientists asked the question to the Project Manager: "Why was Lake County selected as the first county in the nation for monitoring ground water for pesticides?" The

Florida scientists expected a detailed answer with lots of factors and complicated frameworks as they have experienced earlier in Florida.

The Project Manager from Washington, D.C. called and said, "The Lake County was selected because my mother lives there."

Source: Anonymous

A Note – 98

Fred was in the hospital, near death, so the family sent for his pastor . . . . As the pastor stood beside the bed, Fred's frail condition grew worse, and he motioned frantically for something to write on. The pastor lovingly handed him a pen and piece of paper, and Fred used his last ounce of strength to scribble a note. Then he died. The pastor thought it best not to look at the note just then, so he slipped it into his jacket pocket. Several days later, at the funeral, the pastor delivered the eulogy. He realized that he was wearing the same jacket that he'd worn the day Fred died.

"You know," he said, "Fred handed me a note just before he died. I haven't read it, but knowing Fred, I'm sure there's a word of inspiration there for us all."

He unfolded the note and read aloud, "You're standing on my oxygen tube!"

Source: Reference No. 6

Whose Job is it? – 99

This is a story about four people named Everybody, Somebody, Anybody and Nobody. There was an important job to be done and Everybody was sure Somebody would do it. Anybody could have done it, but Nobody did it. Somebody got angry about that, because it was Everybody's job. Everybody thought Anybody could do it but Nobody realized that Everybody wouldn't do it. It ended up that Everybody blames Somebody when Nobody did what Anybody could have done.

Source: Anonymous

PHILOSOPHICAL

Feathers in the Wind - 100

Once there was a Catholic priest who made calls regularly in the home of a young widow. Somebody started passing a rumor. Some busybody began to be suspicious. Two ladies "put two and two together" and began to gossip. Suddenly the young widow died and the community was informed that she had been secretly sick with cancer. Only her priest knew about it. He came regularly to pray for her and to help her. But someone with a dirty mind had started talking. The two ladies who were responsible for it all came to the priest and said, "We are sorry, truly sorry. Why didn't you tell us, Father?" (A priest or a minister frequently cannot defend himself without violating somebody else's confidence.) The priest answered, "All right, if you're sorry, take this feather pillow, go to the top of the hill, and let the feathers fly where the wind will carry them." And they did. When they came back with their empty pillowcase they said, "Father, we have done this. Now, will you forgive us?" The priest answered, "Not until you go out and pick up every feather and put them all back in the sack and bring it back to me." They said, "But that is impossible, Father. The winds have blown the feathers to the four corners." To which he replied, "So it is with your words."

Source: Reference No.1 2

Management 101 - 101

An eagle was sitting on a tree resting, doing nothing. A small rabbit saw the eagle and asked him, "Can I also sit like you and do nothing?"

The eagle answered: "Sure, why not." So, the rabbit sat on the ground below the eagle and rested. All of a sudden, a fox appeared, jumped on the rabbit and ate it.

Management Lesson: To be sitting and doing nothing, you must be sitting very, very high up.

Source: Reference No. 7

The Cracked Pot - 102

A water bearer in India had two large pots, each hung on each end of a pole which he carried across his neck. One of the pots had a crack in it, and while the other pot was perfect and always delivered a full portion of water. At the end of the long walk from the stream to the house, the cracked pot arrived only half full.

For a full two years this went on daily, with the bearer delivering only one and a half pots full of water to his house. Of course, the perfect pot was proud of its accomplishments, perfect to the end for which it was made. But the poor cracked pot was ashamed of its own imperfection, and miserable that it was able to accomplish only half of what it had been made to do. After two years of what it perceived to be a bitter failure, it spoke to the water bearer one day by the stream.

"I am ashamed of myself, and I want to apologize to you. I have been able to deliver only half my load because this crack in my side causes water to leak out all the way back to your house. Because of my flaws, you have to do all of this work, and you don't get full value from your efforts."

The bearer said to the pot, "Did you notice that there were flowers only on your side of your path, but not on the other pot's side? That's because I have always known about your flaw, and I planted flower seeds on your side of the path, and every day while we walk back, you've watered them. For two years I have been able to pick these beautiful flowers to decorate the table. Without you being just the way you are, there would not be this beauty to grace the house."

Moral: Each of us has our own unique flaws. We're all cracked pots. Remember to appreciate all the different people in your life!

Blessings to all my crackpot friends.

Source: Reference No. 7

Why Worry! - 103

There are only two things to worry about. Either you are well, or you are sick. If you are well then there is nothing to worry about. But if you are sick, there are two things to worry about. Either you will get well or you will die. If you get well there is nothing to worry about. If you die there are only two things to worry about. Either you will go to Heaven or Hell. If you go to Heaven, there is nothing to worry about, but if you go to Hell, you'll be so darn busy shaking hands with friends, you won't have time to worry.

Source: Anonymous

THOUGHT PROVOKING

A Monkey Driving the Car - 104

There was a serious accident on an interstate highway in Florida. When policemen arrived at the scene of the accident, police noticed that everyone was dead. Police worried about making the report without any idea of what happened.

While closely observing the car, the police officer noticed a movement in the back seat of the car. There was a live monkey. The policeman worried that the monkey could not speak so evidence could not be gathered, but the cop decided to try anyway. He asked the monkey, "Do you know that a serious accident has taken place?" The monkey nodded his head. The police were encouraged to ask more questions. The policeman asked, "What were the husband, wife and kids doing?" The monkey indicated by acting that the husband was drinking, the wife was talking and the kids were playing in the back seat. Police asked the monkey who was driving. The monkey indicated that he was!

Source: Anonymous

A Monkey with the Torch - 105

When a monkey is given torch, the money gets jubilated and starts jumping from house to house. The houses are burned one by one. The monkey is not cognizant of what is happening, but the monkey is excited with the torch so he jumps from house to house. He is jubilant and gets additional energy to jump faster and longer and tried to enjoy the ride without knowing the consequences.

The homeowners are suffering but the monkey is having the fun of his life… lots of activities (burning) are taking place; surrounding the monkey. That excites the monkey more and more and the monkey jumps over more and more houses in joy without knowing the tragedy.

The monkey with the torch is dangerous to society and the torch should be taken from the monkey to save the neighborhood.

Source: Anonymous

The Ship - 106

A marketing specialist, formerly a sailor, was very aware that ships are addressed as "she" and "her". He often wondered what gender should be used when referring to computers. To answer that question, he set up two groups of computer experts. The first was comprised of women, and the second of men. Each group was asked to recommend whether computers should be referred to in the feminine gender or the masculine gender. They were asked to give 4 reasons for their recommendation.

The group of women reported that the computers should be referred to in the masculine gender because:

In order to get their attention, you have to turn them on.

They have a lot of data, but are still clueless.

They are supposed to help you solve problems, but half the time they are the problem.

As soon as you commit to one, you realize that, if you had waited a little longer you could have had a better model.

The men, on the other hand, concluded that computers should be referred to in the feminine gender because:

No one but the creator understands their internal logic.

The native language they use to communicate with other computers is incomprehensible to everyone else.

Even your smallest mistakes are stored in long-term memory for later retrieval.

As soon as you make a commitment to one, you find yourself spending half your paycheck on accessories for it.

Source: Reference No. 7

Prison vs. Work - 107

IN PRISON you spend the majority of your time in a 10X10, foot cell.

AT WORK you spend the majority of your time in an 8X8 foot cubicle.

IN PRISON you get three meals a day.

AT WORK you get a break for one meal and you have to pay for it.

IN PRISON you get time off for good behavior.

AT WORK you get more work for good behavior.

IN PRISON you can watch TV and play games.

AT WORK you could get fired for watching TV and playing games.

IN PRISON you get your own toilet.

AT WORK you have to share a toilet with some people who pee on the seat.

IN PRISON they allow your family and friends to visit.

AT WORK you aren't even supposed to speak to your family.

IN PRISON all expenses are paid by the taxpayers with no work required.

AT WORK you get to pay all your expenses to go to work, and they deduct taxes from your salary to pay for prisoners.

IN PRISON you spend most of your life inside bars wanting to get out.

AT WORK you spend most of your time wanting to get out and go inside bars.

IN PRISON .you must deal with sadistic wardens.

AT WORK they are called managers.

Source: Reference No. 7

Only in America - 108

Only in America ... can a pizza get to your house faster than an ambulance.

Only in America ... are there handicap parking places in

front of a skating rink.

Only in America ... do people order double cheeseburgers, large fries, and a diet coke.

Only in America ... do banks leave both doors open and then chain the pens to the counters.

Only in America ... do we leave cars worth thousands of dollars in the driveway and put our useless junk in the garage.

Only in America ... do we use answering machines to screen calls and then have call waiting so we won't miss a call from someone we didn't want to talk to in the first place.

Only in America ... do we buy hot dogs in packages of ten and buns in packages of eight.

Only in America ... do we use the word 'politics' to describe the process so well: 'Poli' in Latin meaning 'many' and 'tics' meaning 'bloodsucking creatures'.

Source: Reference No. 6

Sins of Omission - 109

A nursing aid at a retirement home noticed an elderly man sitting by himself in the lounge apparently sunk in deep reflection. "Hello Les, what are you thinking about?" she asked.

I was just thinking about my sins of omission." Les replied somewhat mournfully."What do you mean, your sins of omission?" the aid asked.

"I mean, I've been thinking about the sins I ought to have committed, but didn't."

Source: Reference No. 16

Understanding the 'Stock Market' - 110

Once upon a time in a village somewhere in Asia, a man appeared and announced to the villagers that he would buy monkeys for $5 each. The villagers seeing that there were many monkeys around, went out to the forest, and started catching them. The man bought hundreds at $5 and put the monkeys in a big cage which he had built nearby. As supply started to diminish, the villagers stopped their effort. So he further announced that he would now buy at $10. That renewed the efforts of the villagers and they started catching monkeys again. Soon the supply diminished even further and people started going back to other pursuits. The offer doubled to $20 each and the supply of monkeys became so scarce that it was an effort to even see a monkey, let alone catch it!

The man then announced that he would buy monkeys at an incredibly generous $80! However, since he had to go to the city on some business, his assistant would now buy on behalf of him. In the absence of the man, the assistant told the villagers "Look in the big cage over there at all the monkeys that the man has collected. I will sell them to you at $40 and when the man returns from the city, you can sell them to him for $80 each. You'll double your investment."

The villagers rounded up with all their savings and bought all the monkeys. Then they never saw the man, nor his assistant again - only monkeys everywhere! Now you have a better understanding of how the 'stock market' works.

Source: Reference No. 16

The Explanation of Life - 111

On the first day, God created the cow. God said, "You must go to the field with the farmer all day long and suffer under the sun, have calves and give milk to support the farmer. I will give you a life span of sixty years."

The cow said, "That's a kind of tough life you want me to live for sixty years. Let me have twenty years and I'll give back the other forty." And God agreed.

On the second day, God created the dog. God said, "Sit all day by the door of your house and bark at anyone who comes in or walks past. I will give you a life span of twenty years."

The dog said, "That's too long to be barking. Give me ten years and I'll give back the other ten." So God agreed (sigh).

On the third day God created the monkey. God said, "Entertain people, do monkey tricks, make them laugh. I'll give you a twenty year life span."

Monkey said, "How boring, monkey tricks for twenty years? I don't think so. Dog gave you back ten, so that's what I'll do too, okay?" And God agreed again.

On the fourth day God created man. God said, "Eat, sleep, play, have sex, enjoy. Do nothing, just enjoy, enjoy. I'll give you twenty years."

Man said, "What? Only twenty years? No way man. Tell you what, I'll take my twenty, and the forty cow gave back, and the ten dog gave back and the ten monkey gave back. That makes eighty, okay?" "Okay," said God. "You've got a deal."

So that is why for the first twenty years we eat, sleep, play, have sex, enjoy, and do nothing; for the next forty years we slave in the sun to support our family; for the next ten years we do monkey tricks to entertain our grandchildren; and for the last ten years we sit in front of the house and bark at everybody.

Source: Anonymous

Conundrum - 112

Resolving a conundrum requires reasoning that is not immediately obvious and about ideas that may not be obtainable by using only traditional step-by-step logic. When considering a conundrum, it is important to check your assumptions. You need to be open-minded, flexible and creative in your questioning and able to put lots of different clues and pieces of information together. Once you reach a viable solution, you keep going in order to refine it or replace it with a better solution.

Example 1: A man and his son are in a car crash. The father is killed and the son is taken to a hospital gravely injured. When he gets there, the surgeon says, "I can't operate on this boy, he is my son!" How is this possible?"

Answer 1: The surgeon is the boy's mother. Most people imagine a surgeon as a male, but in this case, it is the opposite! Lateral thinking is the method of switching perceptions to allow the alternative view point.

Example 2: There is a man who lives on the top floor of a very tall building. Everyday he gets the elevator down to the ground floor to leave the building to go to work. Upon returning from work though, he can only travel half of the distance up riding in the elevator and has to walk the rest of the way up unless it's raining! How can this be?

Answer 2: The man in very, very short and can only reach half way up the elevator buttons (assuming the levels of the buttons designating floors increases from bottom to top). However, if it is raining then he will have his umbrella with him and can press the higher buttons using it.

Example 3: Mel Colly stared through the dirty soot-smeared window on the 26th floor of the office tower. Overcome with depression, he slid the window open and jumped through it. It was a sheer drop outside the building to the ground. Miraculously, after he landed, he was completely unhurt. Since there was nothing to cushion his fall or slow his descent, how could he have survived?

Answer 3: Mel Colly was so sick and tired of window washing, he opened the window and jumped inside.

Source: Anonymous

Drunken Observations - 113

Things That Are Difficult To Say When Drunk:
- Innovative
- Preliminary
- Proliferation
- Cinnamon

Things That Are Very Difficulty To Say When Drunk:
- Specificity
- Anti-constitutionalistically

Passive-aggressive disorder

Transubstantiate

Things That Are Downright Impossible To Say When Drunk:

No thanks, I'm married.

Nope, no more booze for me!

Sorry, but you're not really my type

Taco Bell? No thanks, I'm not hungry.

Good evening, officer. Isn't it lovely out tonight?

Oh, I couldn't! No one wants to hear me sing karaoke.

I'm not interested in fighting you.

Thank you, but I won't make any attempt to dance, I have no coordination. I'd hate to look like a fool!

Where is the nearest bathroom? I refuse to pee in this parking lot or on the side of the road.

I must be going home now, as I have to work in the morning.

Source: Reference No. 7

Medical Alert-114

This virus is called Weekly Overload Recreational Killer (WORK).

If you receive WORK from your boss, any of your colleagues or anyone else via any means whatsoever –DO NOT TOUCH IT!!! This virus will wipe out your life entirely. If you should come in contact with WORK you should immediately leave the premises.

Take two good friends to the nearest liquor store and purchase one or both of the antidotes- Work Isolating Neutralizer Extract (WINE) and Bothersome Employer Elimination Rebooter (BEER). Take the antidote repeatedly until WORK has been completely eliminated from your system.

You should immediately forward this medical alert to five friends. If you do not have five friends, you have already been infected and WORK is, sadly controlling your life.

Source: Reference No. 7

Man's Best Friend - 115

A dog is truly a man's best friend. If you don't believe it, just try this experiment.

Put your dog and your spouse in the trunk of the car for an hour. When you open the trunk, who is really happy to see you?

Source: Reference No. 7

REFERENCES

1. Covey Steven R., (1989), "The Seven Habits of Highly Effective People", Fireside, Simon & Schuster Publications, New York.
2. Fellows of the Strategic Studies Group, (1982-83), Naval War College, Newport, Rhode Island.
3. Google search on the internet, 2009.
4. Hart Bruce (1998), Personal Communication.
5. Harvey Paul, "The Rest of the Story", (1996-2001), Paul Harvey Radio Program, FM 107.1, Tallahassee, Florida.
6. Kale Sanjeev, (1998), Personal Communication
7. McAvoy Gene, (1999-2007), " South Florida Vegetable Pest and Disease Hotline" Hendry County Extension office of the Institute of Food and Agriculture sciences of the University of Florida,, P.O. Box 68, Labelle, Florida 33975.
8. Rygiel Paul, (2008), Personal Communication.
9. Schuller Robert H., (1993), "Power Thoughts", HarperCollins publishers, Inc.
10. Schuller Robert H, (2000), a sermon published by the Crystal Cathedral Ministries, Garden Grove, California.
11. Schuller Robert A, (2002), "Robert H. Schuller's life changers", published by the Crystal Cathedral Ministries, Garden Grove, California.
12. Schuller Robert H. (2004), "Hours of Power", daily book of motivation and inspiration, Special 50th Anniversary edition, Crystal Cathedral Ministries, Garden Grove, California.

13. Schuller Robert H, "The Hour of Power", TV program, 1977-2008.

14. Shahane A.N., (1996), "A Potpourri of collective thoughts", Thomas/Ayers Publishing Company, Tallahassee, Florida 32303.

15. Shahane A.N., (1997), "Some practical collective thoughts for daily life", Father and Son Publishing, Inc, Tallahassee, Florida 32303.

16. Summer Peter, (2008) "The Seer–stories", website maintained by Peter Summer, a spiritual mentor based at Gurukula in Fremantle, Western Australia, September-November 2008.

ABOUT THE AUTHOR

Ashok N. Shahane received a Doctorate Degree in Civil and Environmental Engineering from the University of Connecticut in 1973. He is a registered Professional Engineer (P.E.) in the state of Florida since January 1977, a registered Professional Hydrologist (P.H.) since 1986, and a Certified Ground Water Professional (CGWP) since 1985. In 1996 he became a Certified Public Manager (CPM) from the Florida Center for Public Management of the Florida State University in Tallahassee, Florida. He was inducted into the District 47 Hall of Fame in 1989 with the Distinguished Toastmaster award.

Dr. Shahane started his career with the South Florida Water Management District (SFWMD) as an Environmental Systems Engineer. He worked for SFWMD for six years and then he was appointed as Senior Hydrologist and Project Manager for the General Development Corporation in Miami, Florida. For a year, he worked as an Assistant Manager for the AT&T Corporation. He was appointed as a Hydrologist for the Florida Department of Agriculture and Consumer Services in its program of regulating pesticides statewide from January 1984 to March 2008. In March 2008, he was appointed as a Herbicide Registration Coordinator as an Environmental Specialist in the Pesticide Registration Section of the Bureau of Pesticides in the Division of Agricultural Environmental Services. He is listed in Who's Who in Government.

As an Adjunct Professor of Engineering, Hydrology, Hydraulics, and Water Resources, Dr. Shahane taught and introduced several new undergraduate and graduate level courses at the University of Miami, Florida International University in Miami and FAMU/FSU College of Engineering in Tallahassee, Florida from 1979 to 1996. He was invited as a Keynote Speaker for several Annual Meetings and Conferences in Florida.

He is an author of 150 reports and publications, the majority of which have appeared in several reputable and international Journals. He has authored two books which have been published in 1996 and 1997.

In addition to his professional activities, he is a member of Toastmasters International for thirty-four years. He joined Palm Beach Noon Toastmasters in West Palm Beach, Florida to hone his communication skills and develop his leadership talents. He received several awards for his meritorious service and professional work. He has been a winner numerous times for his speeches at various levels in speech contests.